PENGUIN HANDBOOKS

Swimming Skills

Dr. Frank Ryan, who holds a Ph.D.
in psychology, was for many years
varsity field coach at Yale University in
New Haven, Connecticut, where he still lives.
Renowned for his techniques of physical
and mental conditioning in all sports,
he is the author of many respected
and authoritative sports books,
among them *Gymnastics for Girls*,
also a Penguin Handbook.

ALSO BY DR. FRANK RYAN

Discus

Gymnastics for Girls

High Jump

Pole Vault

Shot-Put

Sprint

Weight Training

DR. FRANK RYAN

Swimming Skills

FREESTYLE, BUTTERFLY, BACKSTROKE, BREASTSTROKE

PENGUIN BOOKS

Penguin Books Ltd, Harmondsworth,
Middlesex, England
Penguin Books, 625 Madison Avenue,
New York, New York 10022, U.S.A.
Penguin Books Australia Ltd, Ringwood,
Victoria, Australia
Penguin Books Canada Limited, 2801 John Street,
Markham, Ontario, Canada L3R 1B4
Penguin Books (N.Z.) Ltd, 182–190 Wairau Road,
Auckland 10, New Zealand

Freestyle Swimming first published in the United States of America
by The Viking Press 1972
Butterfly Swimming first published in the United States of America
by The Viking Press 1974
Backstroke Swimming first published in the United States of America
by The Viking Press 1974
Breaststroke Swimming first published in the United States of America
by The Viking Press 1974
Published in one volume in Penguin Books 1978
Reprinted 1979

Freestyle Swimming copyright © Frank Ryan, 1972
Butterfly Swimming copyright © Frank Ryan, 1974
Backstroke Swimming copyright © Frank Ryan, 1974
Breaststroke Swimming copyright © Frank Ryan, 1974
Compilation copyright © Frank Ryan, 1978
All rights reserved

LIBRARY OF CONGRESS CATALOGING IN PUBLICATION DATA
Ryan, Frank.
Swimming skills.
Contains revised versions of the author's Freestyle swimming,
Butterfly swimming, Backstroke swimming, and Breaststroke swimming.
1. Swimming.   I. Title.
[GV837.R885]   797.2'1   78-5155
ISBN 0 14 046.338 0

Printed in the United States of America by
Halliday Lithograph Corporation, West Hanover, Massachusetts
Set in Caledonia

All illustrations by courtesy of Ryan Films, Inc.
Copyright © Ryan Films, Inc., 1963, 1969, 1970, 1972

Contents

Author's Note

I always like to have an informal word with the reader, but in some ways this is perhaps the most difficult writing of all. In putting together this book, I have constantly tried to visualize you. I have had so many years of face-to-face coaching in athletics that now I can think only of the person I am coaching. In this book that's you. Therefore you'll understand the informal approach of this book. It sometimes is more formal, but only when that seems the helpful way to get across an idea.

Each book in my series is based on a carefully researched athletic instructional film. Actual photos from the films are reproduced in these books. In making the films I have always sought the cooperation of the best experts, and all the experts have responded enthusiastically.

The expert consultant on all films on swimming has been Phil Moriarty, Head Coach of Swimming at Yale University. Despite his long coaching day, Phil has found time to make sure the films embodied the best of teaching. With this book he has been equally vigilant in making sure that the best knowledge of backstroke swimming is at your disposal.

Many long conferences were needed to produce this book. Vital to each conference was the presence of Robert J. Reid. Bob Reid supervised the filming of our motion picture and has selected the photos for this book. He is not only a great film man but also a natural teacher with an enthusiasm for participation in sports, especially swimming.

We hope, and we believe, that this book will increase both your enjoyment of swimming and your achievement.

Yale swimming coach Phil Moriarty.   Photographer Bob Reid.

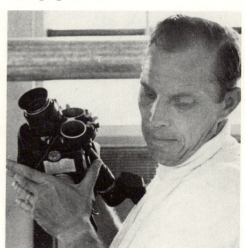

I. Freestyle Swimming

Introduction

Modern swimming techniques have had a remarkably short history. Presently used styles are the products of very recent times. Today's competitive swimmers would look strikingly different from even the champions of the early part of this century. In contrast, the distance runner of today would resemble the runner of ancient times.

It is appropriate to compare swimming and running. They have borrowed much from each other in formulating conditioning views. By now their training methods are quite similar.

All parts of the earth are covered by either land or water. Without mechanical aid, or strictly on his own, man has the potential of movement on land or through the water. The words *on* land and *through* water are significant. Man does move *through* water—not *on* it. That's because the specific gravity of the human body is very close to that of water. This fact has no doubt had an enormous influence on the story of man and the water. The story would have been different if all men had great natural buoyancy —and different again if nobody could float. As things are, man's actions in the water are critical. They decide whether he sinks or swims.

Even though three-quarters of the earth's surface is covered by water, man has been primarily a creature of the land. More than a billion people have lived and died without having swum a single stroke. Even today, many millions of people cannot swim. Yet every able-bodied person can move about the land by walking or running.

It seems puzzling that it took mankind so long to develop efficient swimming techniques. You would think that man would have learned to swim well even before he learned to speak or develop a culture. The water was always there for him.

Much of the explanation for man's early failure to swim proficiently probably lies in the nature of a good part of the surrounding water. A lot of the water is rough, cold, or otherwise dangerous. However, in certain parts of the world the waters are ideal for inducing man to enter them. Not only are the conditions for swimming good, but there are tangible rewards in the forms of fish and shellfish. The ideal spots seem to be in the South Seas Islands.

The South Seas Islanders were rewarded in their food-seeking efforts in the surrounding waters. In addition, the fun-loving and relaxed temperament of the natives played a part. They enjoyed the activity of swimming and became good at it. They actually developed a form of the crawl stroke.

The next link in the historic chain came about because of the nearness of Australia to the Islands. Possibly the most sporting people in the world, the Australians were especially fond of swimming. The Australian swimmers observed the methods of the islanders. They then adopted and refined what they saw. The swimming revolution had started.

The roots were there, but three more contributions were needed to bring swimming performance to its present level. First, smooth water is necessary for highly efficient speed swimming. Open water is simply too rough. The construction of well-engineered pools has been a critical part of modern swimming history. Happily, more and more pools are being built.

Second, there has been the emergence of professional swimming coaches. Able and dedicated, these men spent countless hours in improving their sport. All phases of swimming were constantly analyzed. They looked especially to the physical sciences to yield refinements and ideas on the mechanics of swimming. Within this framework they carried on bold and fruitful experiments.

Third, swimming has been participating in a "conditioning revolution" that has been affecting all sports. Until about a generation ago our training schedules were based largely on intuition and guesswork. It turned out that we badly underestimated the optimum amounts of work. Physiological research has drastically revised our notions of what a workout should be.

Swimming is an exciting sport. Its progress in the past fifty years outstrips the advances made in the previous million years. The application of modern science and thinking has made the difference. But, first and foremost, swimming is a sport—and it's fun. Perhaps no other sports activity is more rewarding to the participant.

Approach to Form

In a freestyle race you can, by definition, use any style that you want. If you liked you could begin with one stroke and switch to another during the race. But, as a practical matter, you would stay entirely with the crawl stroke, because it is the fastest stroke yet devised.

What is good sprint-crawl form? How do we judge it? By good form we mean the use of the body and its parts to move through the water as efficiently as possible. Hence there should really be nothing mysterious about good form. In general, our notions of good form derive from two bases—experience and theory. Many new techniques have been tried by coaches and swimmers over the generations. The innovations that seemed to work well have been retained and used. Others have been discarded. So some of our present teachings were evolved by trial and error. We profit from the experience of countless swimmers.

As in many other athletic events, our present ideas of swimming form have been shaped by theoretical considerations including physical principles. We can deduce points that seem likely to offer improvement. When both practical experience and theory are in agreement, we can have a high level of confidence in our views.

Let's approach the problem of sprint crawl in a simple and systematic way. Suppose we consider a model (photo series 1) that could represent any floating body. If this body is to move through the water, what factors will determine its speed? How fast our model will move depends upon (photo #1a) its power plant, (photo #1b) the amount of resistance that the body offers to the water, and (photo #1c) the efficiency of propulsion.

If we think in terms of a boat, we can easily visualize each of the three factors that affect speed. Other things equal, a boat with a high-powered engine will move faster than one with less power. But the engine has to be in good condition. Otherwise, it won't make the contribution to speed that it should.

Resistance always exists whenever a body moves through the water. A boat's bow has to push water aside. Its stern tends to drag water with it. Some resistance is inevitable, but marine engineers try to design boats so that this resistance is reduced as much as possible.

Efficiency of propulsion is the remaining factor in determining speed. Power should be applied so that it best brings about forward movement. It is possible to use enormous power without getting much propulsion from it. In fact, poor use of power could cause the body to remain motionless or even move backward.

What applies to all floating bodies generally applies to the swimmer. He conditions his "power plant." He must be strong and in excellent physical condition. He tries for a streamline body position that will minimize water resistance. He learns swimming techniques that will propel him efficiently. Swimming, however, does have a realistic complication. Unlike the boat, the swimmer must use a substantial part of his body for propulsion. In other words, for the swimmer the reduction of body resistance and the efficiency of propulsion are related. Some streamlining has to be sacrificed to get better propulsion.

1. A body's speed through the water depends upon (1a) its power plant, (1b) the resistance it offers to the water, (1c) the efficiency of propulsion.

1a

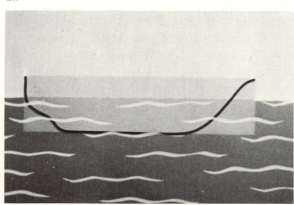

1b

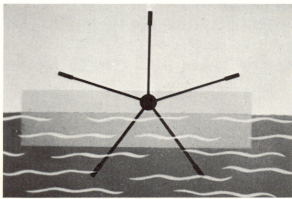

1c

Body Position

The less resistance that your body offers to the water the faster you will move. The human body isn't very streamlined compared to that of a fish, but there is still a lot that we can do to lessen drag. Body position in the water can have great effect on the amount of resistance.

Let's suppose that you are holding on to a rope and being towed through the water at a constant speed. As you assume different body positions you would feel different amounts of pull or pressure on the rope. The amount of pull you felt would indicate the amount of drag your body was creating. The greatest resistance would be felt with your body in a vertical position. The least resistance would occur when your body becomes straight and flat.

You can see that you'll move best when your body lies in a flat position. The body should be almost parallel to the surface of the water. Your body cannot be completely parallel, however, because your feet have to be deep enough to kick effectively. The head and chest are a little higher than the lower body. The position of the head puts the hairline about even with the surface of the water. The head is comfortably held in alignment with the body. The shoulders are at right angles to the line of the body.

Training in correct breathing starts at the poolside. You learn to bob up and down taking a deep breath above the water and then to drop below the water to force out the air. The bobbing up and down is carried out with an easy rhythm. Most of the time is spent under water in expiration.

The ratio is about five to one—that is, for every second that the head is above the surface it is submerged for about five seconds.

Inhalation is through the mouth. And it is rapid. There just isn't much time to take in a breath. You breathe out through both your nose and mouth. Though you have to inhale quickly, there is much more time to exhale. Air can be expelled smoothly and easily.

You can breathe without lifting your head. You can put yourself into position to breathe with an easy twisting of your neck. The reason you can do this is that the head creates a bow wave. The water is pushed aside, and there is a trough or "hole" in the water. The head rotates smoothly so that a breath can be taken at the bottom of the depression. In this way the head doesn't have to be lifted very much, and there is only a slight interference with streamlined body position. Rotation of the head is the key to efficient breathing. Rotation serves two purposes. The head does not have to be lifted, and the body does not have to be turned.

The rotation of the head need not and certainly should not be forced or artificial. The rotation should be smoothly and easily coordinated with body rotation. During each stroke the body has a natural tendency to roll to one side. The head should roll in the same direction.

In the short sprint races very few inhalations are needed. A trained sprinter can swim a full pool length with only several breaths. In the longer races it is common practice to take in a breath with every second stroke.

After starting, it is best that no breaths be taken during the first few strokes. This is the time when good body position is established. If the head does not have to be turned, a streamlined body position is easier to attain.

The first approach to getting good body position is to visualize it—to have a clear picture and then to try directly for it. This is the positive way. However, it's realistic to know that the body can get out of alignment along any one of three axes, even if it is straight. When we speak of these three possibilities for error we mean that (1) the body could fail to be flat enough, (2) the body could be sideways, and (3) the body could be rolling too much. Let's look at each.

Of the three possible errors the most common is the failure to maintain a level position in the water. Usually this comes from trying to lift the head too high with a resulting dropping of the lower body. In most cases this error can be eliminated by emphasis on correct breathing habits. Failure to kick sufficiently can also drop the lower body. We'll be talking about this when we get to the subject of leg action.

A swinging of the body from side to side increases water resistance or drag. This lateral movement can have a number of roots. Movement of the head out of alignment will tend to drive the body sideways. Correct arm action is essential to keeping good body position. Lateral movement of the arms tends to produce lateral movement of the body. Though any phase of the stroke may contribute to poor body alignment, lateral motion seems to be more common during recovery. Many swimmers have difficulty swinging their arms in a vertical plane. This error usually comes from lack of flexibility. Special exercises may be needed.

The legs have a strong effect on body alignment. Their action on the downbeat overcomes the tendency on the lower body to sink. In this way the legs help keep the body flat. But leg action also greatly influences lateral alignment. Faulty kicking could throw the body from side to side, but for the most part leg action tends to preserve alignment. The legs almost automatically kick slightly sideways to compensate for lateral forces introduced by the arms or head.

A rolling about the long axis of the body increases water resistance. Though a completely stable body position would produce less drag, a certain amount of roll is both inevitable and needed. With a rolling motion the arms can pull more effectively, and breathing can be carried out easier. You should not make a direct effort to roll, but don't try to stop the roll either. Let it come naturally.

How *high* should you ride in the water? There seems to be considerable concern with this question, but not much can or should be done about it. Theoretically, the higher you are in the water the faster you will go, and, conversely, the faster you move the higher you will be in the water. However, at swimming speed the amount of lift that the body receives is not significant. Efforts to ride higher in the water are not only useless—they are damaging. Direct efforts to lift the body interfere with both alignment and efficient propulsion.

How high you swim depends primarily on your natural buoyancy. Muscle and bone are relatively heavy. Most fine sprinters are big-boned and heavily muscled. This means a high specific gravity. Hence many good sprinters cannot even float. So don't worry about your height in the water.

In summary, body position is a highly significant factor in swimming. Drag must be reduced as much as possible. You start by being aware of the need for good position, and you try to visualize what this position should be. Nonalignment has to be checked along three axes—up and down, sideways, and extreme rolling. With increased experience your own feelings about the position of your body will become more and more reliable. You will get to feel or sense unnecessary water resistance. But, whenever possible, get the observations of your coach. Body position should be checked regularly. If needed, you and your coach can figure out the corrective action that should be taken.

2. A flat, streamlined body position cuts down water resistance. The legs are slightly lower than the upper body to permit effective kicking. Note (e and f) that the head turns so that breathing can be carried out without disturbing body position.

2d

2a

2e

2b

2f

2c

3. Poolside training in correct breathing. Breaths are taken quickly. Five times as much time is spent under water in exhaling.

4. Intake of air actually takes place in the trough or "hole" created by the bow wave.

3*a*

4

3*b*

Arms

The arms supply most of the forward propulsion. Some experts think that the arms supply all or nearly all of swimming power. This position is probably an extreme position, but the great importance of arm action is entirely clear. The arms are not as strong as the legs. The enormous contribution to forward movement made by the arms comes mainly from their flexibility, including the fact they can be taken out of the water during recovery. The flexibility of the arms permits much of their effort to be applied efficiently. We will be looking at this efficiency. During recovery the arms are brought back through the air rather than the water. For this reason there is greater arm speed, and much less water resistance is created.

All aspects of swimming are important to great performance, but if we had to single out one aspect as the most important, it would be arm action. This action must be efficient. It has to be understood, learned, and ingrained. Champions may have differences in some things they do, but all have good arm action. Their smooth and efficient strokes contrast sharply with the wild arm thrashings of the novice.

So that we can take a clear and logical look at the chief features of arm action, let's examine a simple model (photo series 6). We illustrate with a model of an old-fashioned paddle wheel. Actually, the hand and forearm act like a paddle.

In our model suppose we isolate one paddle and follow this single paddle through a cycle. We can then examine the effect on forward propulsion of various positions.

When the paddle first enters the water (photos 6a, b) its action is mostly downward, and therefore the reaction is mostly upward. The force supplies a lot of lift but very little forward power. So you can see that, at this point in the stroke, much of the power is being wasted.

As the stroke proceeds (photo 6c) the lifting action becomes less, and the forward drive is increased. Efficiency is improving.

At that point where the paddle is straight down (photo 6d), efficiency reaches its peak. Push is directly backward, and for this reason all force is directed forward.

Now as the paddle moves past the vertical (photo 6e), it begins to push upward as well as backward. While at this point there is still a good backward push, there is also an upward push. Much of the energy is used in driving the body downward. Toward the completion of the stroke the force exerted by the paddle causes the boat to be pulled downward. Power is wasted. Efficiency is low.

Our model shows what happens when we have a fixed or rigid paddle. Only a brief portion of the stroke can be highly efficient. There is much waste. But suppose we have a way of changing the shape of the paddle during its stroke. Suppose we have a joint that allows a substantial portion of the paddle to be bent. This ability to bend makes a big difference. Now look at the early portion of the stroke (photo 7a). The bending allows the action to be more directly backward and, therefore, the reaction to be more directly forward. The efficiency of the first part of the stroke is greatly increased. We can, in fact, by bending the paddle, maintain an effective forward force during most of the stroke (photo series 7a–d). We can take our paddle model and easily translate its action into what it means for swimming. We know at once that stiff arms will not be efficient in propelling the body through the water. We know that the arms will have to bend during the stroke, and we know that the amount of bend is going to depend on the part of the stroke.

As you move your arm through the water, you can control the angle made by your upper and lower arm. In other words, a bending of the elbow can put the forearm in a better position to push backward throughout all phases of the stroke. Also, you can control the angle formed by your wrist and hand. By adjusting this angle the hand can be kept perpendicular to the surface of the water throughout the greater part of the stroke.

In summary, the flexion of your elbow and that of your wrist is used to push the water as directly backward as possible. The more directly you can drive the water backward, the more efficiently you drive your body straight ahead.

There is still another reason for flexing the elbow during the early part of the pull. The lever arm is shortened. Mechanical advantage is increased and more force can be exerted against the water. This is the same principle that permits a car to start faster in low gear. During the first part of the stroke the elbow should be higher than the hand. In this way both power and efficiency of propulsion are greater.

Action and reaction are in opposite directions. The direction in which the hand pushes the water is of great importance, because the body tends to move in the opposite direction. That's why the hands should move directly backward as much as possible. In this way the reaction pushes the body forward. Deviations from backward action of the hands tend to move the body sideways.

Arm action is alternate, that is, one arm pulls while the other recovers. It is not enough for the arms to move parallel to the body. Alternate pulls could produce lateral motion. So the pulling action is not only in alignment with forward direction. It is also beneath the center of the body.

Ideally, the stroke should satisfy two main requirements. First, you try to push the water directly backward. You do this by adjusting the angle made by your upper and lower arm and the angle made by your wrist and hand. Second, the path of your hand is directly under your body's center of gravity. Because of the body's construction the hand does not actually travel backward in a straight line. The path of the hand tends to be somewhat circular. The hand crosses the center line of the body and then comes back.

Recovery. When the arm completes a stroke, it has to be brought back or to recover so that another stroke can be started. Action is continuous. As the hand leaves the water at the end of the stroke it is moving fast and in a circular path. It is circular because the hand has to move outward to clear the body. If the arm were straight back, it would take considerable energy and time to reverse the backward movement and get the arm moving forward again. The rotary movement is utilized so that the momentum can be retained.

During the early part of the recovery the elbow leads the way. The hand starts to catch up so that it is about even with the elbow when it reaches shoulder level. From that point on the hand accelerates in a natural and unrushed fashion so that it enters the water first. Upon entering the water the palm is downward and at an angle to the surface. The elbow is partly bent.

The path of the recovery should as much as possible be in the vertical plane. The action should be upward and forward rather than sideways and forward. A sideways recovery of the arm tends to move the body sideways, thus throwing the body out of alignment. If there is continued trouble in making the recovery in the vertical plane, it may be due to tightness. Special exercises to increase shoulder flexibility may be needed.

The recovery can and should be a relaxed and smooth movement. The energy that you use to bring your arm out of the water will usually be enough to keep the arm moving forward. Once the arm is out of the water you apply just enough energy to control its path. This gives you a chance to relax your arms and thus reduce fatigue.

5*a*

5. As the hand enters the water the wrist bends. In this way the hand can push backward.

5*b*

5*c*

6. A cycle of a straight paddle. When the paddle first enters the water (a) its action is almost entirely downward. Hence the reaction shown by the solid arrow (b) is upward. By (c) the reaction is in a more backward direction and therefore more efficient. At (d) where the paddle is pointed directly downward the stroke is most efficient. The entire action is backward. As the cycle continues (e), the action becomes increasingly inefficient. More and more the reaction is in a downward direction.

6*a*

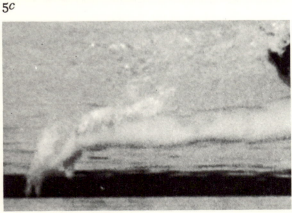

5*d*

6*b*

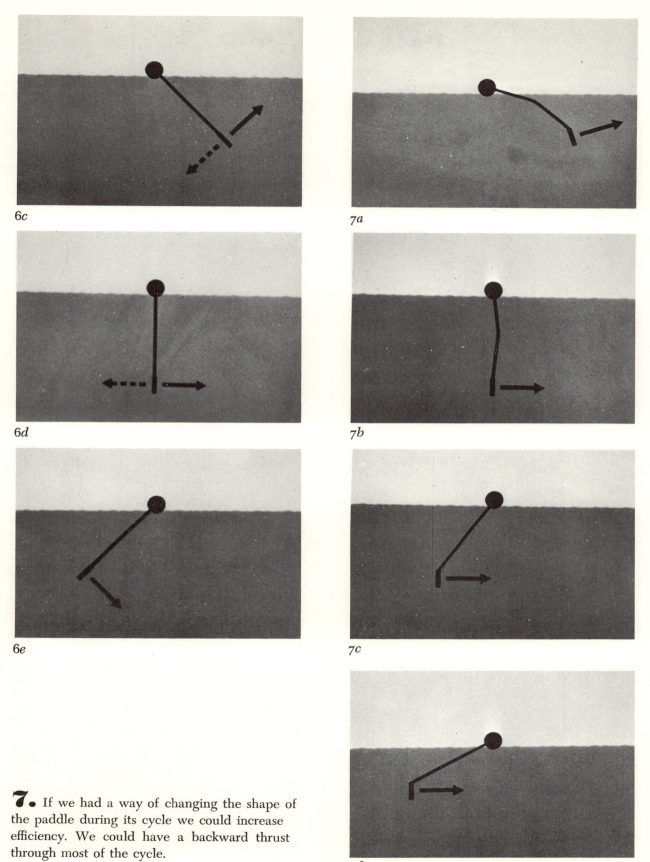

6c

6d

6e

7a

7b

7c

7d

7. If we had a way of changing the shape of the paddle during its cycle we could increase efficiency. We could have a backward thrust through most of the cycle.

8a

8b

8. and **9.** Compare the dry-land series and the underwater sequence with the diagrams in series 7. By bending his elbows and wrists the swimmer greatly increases the efficiency of his arm action. He is able to push backward through much of the stroke.

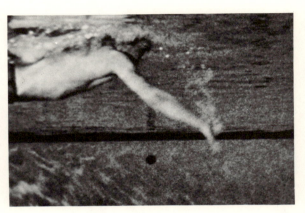

9a

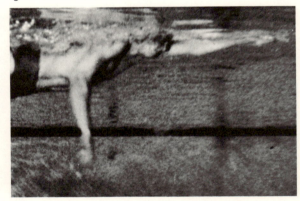

9b

8c

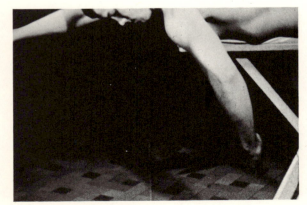

8d

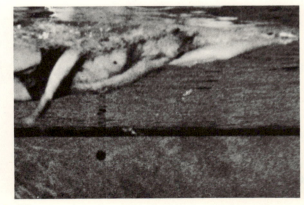

9c

10a

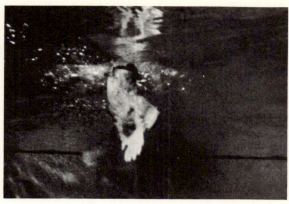

11a

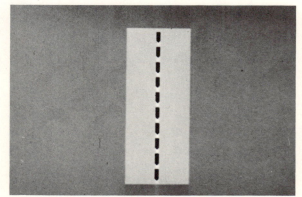

10b

11b

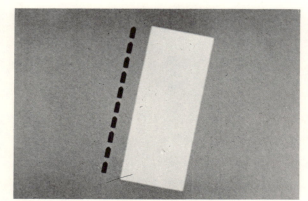

10c

11c

10. It's not enough for the stroke to be parallel to the body. The arms pull alternately. Action that is only parallel would drive the body from side to side (a and b). Hence the path of the stroke should be under the body.

11. The hand actually crosses the center line of the body. Its path is somewhat curved.

11d

12.

12a

12b

12c

12d

13. Recovery. In (a) the elbow is leading the recovery. By (b) the lower arm has caught up to the upper arm. The forearm then goes ahead of the elbow (c). The recovery action is smooth, rhythmic, and relaxed. The initial action of pulling the arm out of the water should supply the momentum for the entire recovery.

13a

13b

13c

Legs

The legs, though stronger than the arms, contribute less to the forward propulsion of the body. Some coaches contend that the only function of the legs is to help stabilize the body. This position is extreme. It surely is theoretically and practically possible to derive forward propulsion from the kick. In fact, it is essential to get a contribution from the legs in order to do your best.

It's helpful to take a look at the theoretical problem of propulsion. For any part of the body to add to forward speed it must be moving *backward* through the water faster than the body is moving forward. Suppose we take a specific example. If the body is moving through the water at a rate of five feet per second, and, at the same time, a part of the body (the foot, for example) is moving backward in relation to the body at four feet per second, what is the situation? Though the part is moving backward in relation to the body, it is actually moving forward in relation to the water—and at a rate of one foot per second. Under this condition the part makes no contribution to forward movement. Quite the opposite. A drag is created.

Put another way, we have to make a distinction between "relative" and "absolute" movement. Suppose you are climbing a ladder in an elevator that is slowly descending. Assume that you are climbing at the rate of four feet per second and the elevator is going down at five feet per second. You would be going upward in relation to the elevator, but you would be going downward in relation to the earth. Your "absolute" speed is one foot per second in a downward direction—even though you are climbing. So it is with swimming. You could move your feet backward in a relative sense and not create propulsion. Movement of the feet has to be fast enough to be "absolute."

For the kick to be truly effective you have to build up to considerable backward foot speed. A distinction between "speed" and "force" is important. Actually, there can be force without any motion. You can push hard against a brick wall without moving it. In swimming it would be possible to apply tremendous force without contributing to propulsion. Speed has to be there too.

Even some of the experts have spread some confusion about the contribution of the kick. They reason as follows. If you swim with your legs tied you will move at a certain rate. This rate represents the contribution of the arms to speed. Now if you eliminate the arm action by using a kickboard, your legs will propel you forward, but at less speed than that of the arms alone. The false reasoning becomes this. If the arms can, for example, move the body forward at a speed of four feet per second and the legs move the body at two feet per second, the resulting speed has to be something like three feet per second. In this way the legs do more harm than good. But, of course, this is not necessarily so. It depends on how fast the feet are moving backward. If they can move backward faster than the arms alone can pull the body forward, then the kick makes a positive contribution. Total speed can be increased. The critical point is not centered about the speed at which the legs can drive a kickboard. It's a matter of how fast the feet can move backward.

In addition to speed, leg action has to be correct. In order to get a simple and rational view of what leg action should be, let's consider the up-and-down movement of a stiff leg (photo 15a). On the downward drive (photo 15b) the pressure on the water is partly down and partly backward. During this phase there is some forward component to the reaction (photo 15c).

At that point where the straight leg is parallel to the water's surface (photo 15d), the pressure is entirely downward. Hence the reaction is entirely upward (photo 15e). A lifting force is created, but there is no contribution to forward propulsion.

Toward the end of the downstroke (photo 15g) the reaction is upward and backward. There is a negative force or interference with forward propulsion.

On the upstroke of the leg the forces are reversed from those of the downstroke. During the first part of the upstroke, the reaction is forward and down (photo 15h). At the midpoint (photo 15i) the reaction is down only. Toward the end of the upstroke (photo 15j) the leg produces a force that is both backward and down.

If the legs were kept rigid their up-and-down movement would result in a cancellation of forces. Any forward force generated would be balanced by an equal backward force. There would, in fact, be a loss because of the drag produced. It is clear that stiff legs cannot contribute to forward propulsion.

We can analyze the above demonstration to see at what points forward propulsion is supplied. We note that there is forward power on the downstroke only before the leg reaches a horizontal position. We can say that on the downstroke there is a contribution to forward propulsion when the angle made by the leg and a horizontal line is greater than zero (photo 15k). Conversely, on the upbeat forward impetus is given to the body only when this angle is less than zero (photo 15l). So in order to get the legs to contribute to forward drive we want to reproduce these conditions. To do so one or more flexible joints are needed. Through flexibility the condition needed for forward propulsion can be met throughout the downstroke. Also, flexibility permits forward drive during the upstroke (photos 15m, n, o).

We can now see the importance of looseness, particularly a loose ankle. If the ankle is loose enough, pressure of the water against the ankle will automatically bring about the adjustments in the angle needed for propulsion. Looseness of the ankle will permit the foot to act as a flipper.

We have emphasized the ankle and foot. It's because the extremities of the limbs move faster. For example, if you swing your arm, your wrist and hand will move faster than your upper arm. The upper arm and muscles of the body supply nearly all of the power, but the speed is in the lower arm. In the same way, though the body and the upper legs supply the real power, what finally matters is the speed of the lower legs and feet.

Now we can summarize what the legs have to do. There are two big factors—speed and angle. The feet must move quickly, and they must push the water as directly backward as possible.

Leg action stabilizes. In addition to contributing to forward propulsion the legs have another important function—that of helping to keep the body stable. Their action aids in sustaining alignment and in keeping the body streamlined. It does so in both the vertical and lateral planes.

There is always a tendency for the lower part of the body to sink. The kick overcomes this dropping tendency and helps to preserve streamlining. The downbeat is a more powerful action than the upbeat. This greater pressure of the downward kick should develop enough force to keep the legs up.

The tendency for the body to move laterally or from side to side varies among swimmers. Much of the weaving can be counteracted by lateral action of the legs. This corrective, partially sideways thrust of the legs is usually carried out almost instinctively and without conscious effort. However, if excessive correction by the legs is needed, the upper body and arm action should be examined. They are introducing too much lateral action.

14. The kick serves two important purposes. It contributes to propulsion. Perhaps just as important, the kicking action helps stabilize the body and in this way it cuts down on drag.

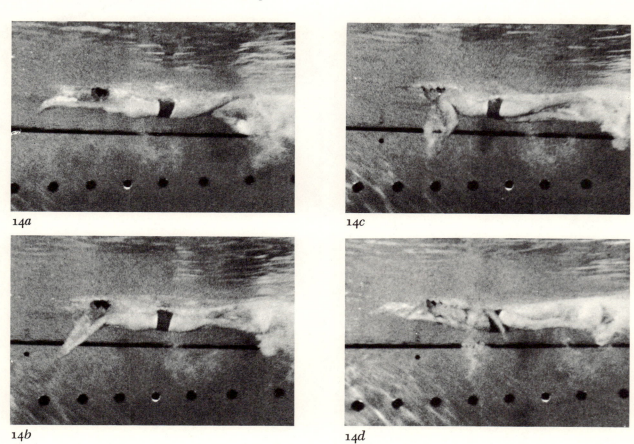

14a

14b

14c

14d

15. Why stiff legs cannot contribute to propulsion. Assume we have two straight legs that move up and down (a). We isolate a single leg and follow its action to see what it does. In (b) the leg is starting downward. The dotted arrow shows the direction of the action. The reaction (solid arrow in c) is partly forward. There is some contribution to forward movement.

(d) Action is directly downward.

(e) Reaction is upward. There is a lifting action at this point.

(f) Downward past the vertical. Action is down and slightly forward.

(g) Reaction is upward, but also slightly backward.

(h, i, j) On the upward stroke the forces are reversed.

(k) On the downstroke forward impetus is given when the angle made by the leg and the horizontal is greater than zero.

(l) On the upstroke there is a forward contribution when the angle is less than zero.

(m, n, o) It takes one or more flexible joints to create the conditions for forward impetus throughout most of the kick.

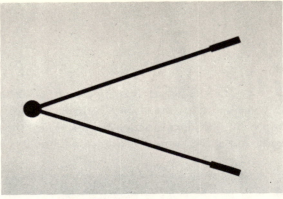

15a

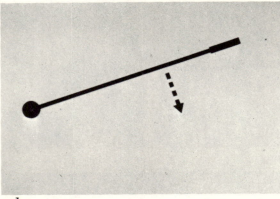

15b

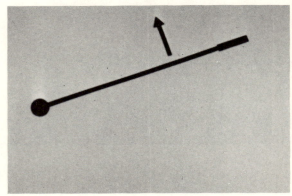

15c

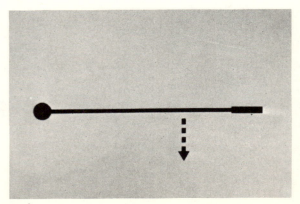

15d

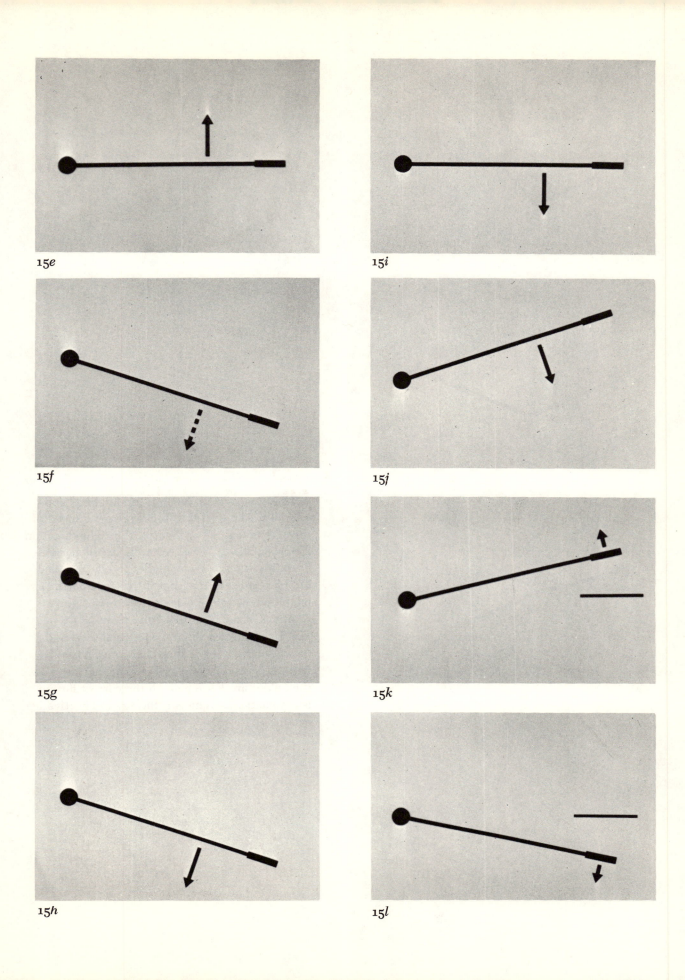

15e

15i

15f

15j

15g

15k

15h

15l

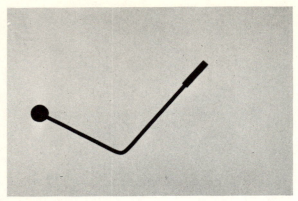

15m

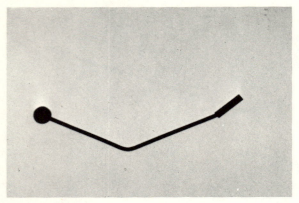

15n

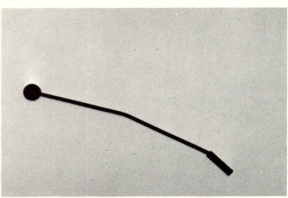

15o

16. Leg action is loose, undulating, and whiplike. The goal is to build up great speed of the feet and to have them in the right direction for a backward thrust. Note the excellent ankle flexibility. Photo #1 is highly significant. The bubbles indicate the velocity of the foot in its final downward movement. Compare the positions of the right foot from photo #1 to #2. In photo #2 the upbeat has started and flexion of the foot is the other way. A similar pattern is seen in other photos in the series. If the ankles are loose enough the correct flexion is automatic. Looseness is the key to effective leg action.

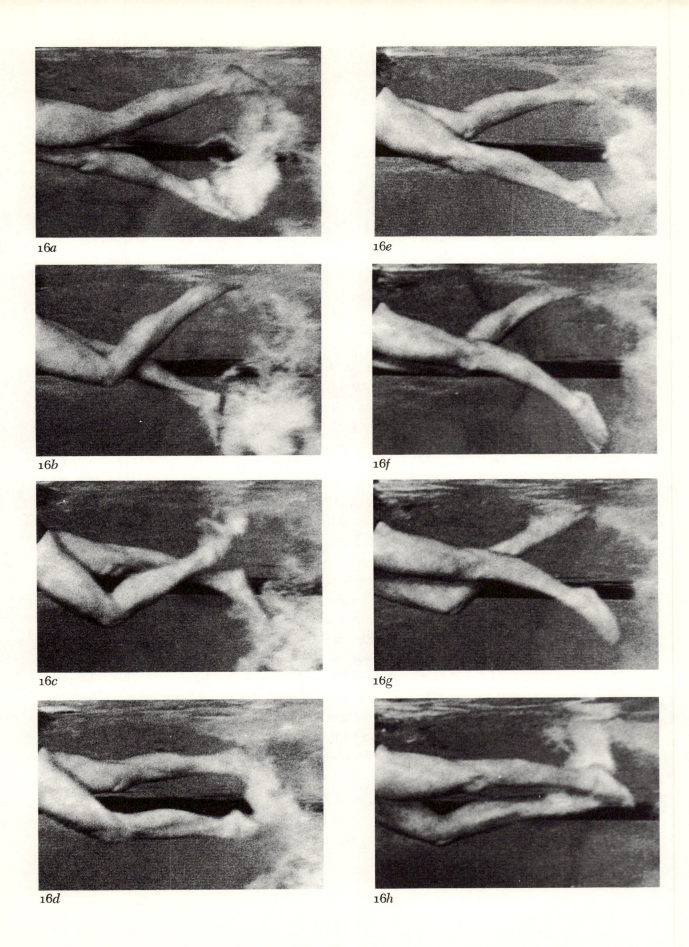

16a

16b

16c

16d

16e

16f

16g

16h

The Start

First, let's consider the old traditional starting form and then talk later about the newer grab start. Except for initial position, the principles and goals are similar. For this reason our illustrations will come mostly from the traditional start. But the grab start should be kept in mind.

The start has enormous and obvious importance in the sprint race. Where inches often mean victory, you cannot afford anything other than the best start that you can make.

The goals of the start are clear. You want to (1) get away fast, (2) generate a powerful forward thrust, (3) enter the water in such a way as to preserve forward momentum, and (4) establish an initial underwater position that maintains speed.

The toes should curl over the edge of the platform. The grip of the toes helps keep balance and affords a firmer contact for the leg drive. The distance between the feet is about six inches or more—the exact spacing depending on the width of the hips. While waiting for the command, "Take your mark," you want to be relaxed but alert.

At the starter's call of "Take your mark," you bend forward to assume a crouched position. The knees are partially bent. Your arms hang easily. Weight is forward and balanced over the balls of your feet. At the sound of the gun, two main things happen. Your arms begin to swing, and your body moves forward and downward.

Push-off position. A track fan seeing his first swimming meet would be aghast at what would seem an eternity between the sound of the gun and the swimmer actually leaving the platform. He is used to seeing the runner leave the blocks and get underway almost with the sound of the gun. He may wonder why the swimmer doesn't do the same thing. Well, the swimmer could spring at the sound of the gun, but in doing so he would get a most inefficient start. His body position would not be right.

Just before the legs make their final drive the body is stretched out and almost horizontal. At this point, the body's center of gravity is not much higher than the starting platform (photo 20f). You can see the logic of attaining such a position. The job is to drive forward, so the body should be pointed forward. If the final drive were to be made with the body fairly erect, the body would be driven upward rather than forward.

How does the body get into position for the final drive? By gravity! When the gun sounds, you drop your head and flex your ankles. In this way you give up your stable position on the platform and start to fall. You cannot do anything to speed up the falling process. You'll drop at the same rate as any other falling body.

Arms. While you are falling, your arms build up momentum. They have time to do it. The arms swing vigorously upward and complete a full circle. The arms have completed a full cycle and are moving forward just as you are ready to make your final drive from the starting platform. As the arms approach the horizontal they are stopped. The energy developed by the arms is not wasted. This energy is transferred to the body and helps its forward motion.

Entry. When the body enters the water it should be as streamlined as possible. Ideally, the body should form a straight line from the tips of the fingers right through to the toes. There should be no protruding parts. The head is between the arms. The hands enter the water first. The body is held stiff so that the impact of the water does not alter the streamlined position of the body. In summary, a knifelike entry is the goal.

The effectiveness of the start also depends on the angle at which the water is entered. Acquiring the optimum angle takes practice and experience. Too steep an angle of entry would drive you too deep. By the time you reached the surface your competitors would be well on their way. At the other extreme, a very flat dive would dissipate valuable energy against the water.

Glide. After you enter the water you must keep calm and maintain your streamlined body position. In the excitement of a race it's hard to keep in mind that an attempt to start swimming right away can actually slow you down. The initial speed that you develop by driving from a solid surface is greater than swimming speed. It takes patience and experience to hold position until the speed of the glide slows down to swimming speed.

The legs begin their drive first, since their movement interferes less with the streamlining of the body. Initial arm action emphasizes back thrust so that you are not drawn to the surface too soon. The breath is held for several strokes to allow body position to be established.

Attention. You will, of course, be attentive and alert as you await the gun. It's not the time for anyone's mind to wander. However, there are two basic orientations for your attention. You can be concentrating on the sound of the gun or you can be thinking of movement. Research shows that your reaction will be faster if your attention is on what you are going to do.

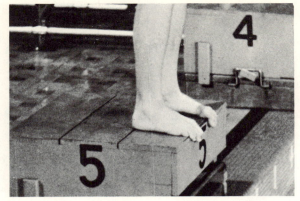

17

18

17. and **18.** The toes are wrapped around the edge of the starting platform.

19. Legs slightly bent. Body weight forward over the balls of the feet.

19

20. (a) "Take your mark" position.
  (b) At the gun, arms start to swing. Weight moves forward.
  (c) Body falling forward. Arms have picked up speed.
  (d, e, f) Body continues to lower and move forward. Legs getting ready to spring.
  (g) Arms now being checked. Momentum is transferred to body.
  (h) Legs drive as body approaches the horizontal.
  (i) Entry.

20*a*

20*b*

20c

20d

20e

20f

20g

20h

20i

21. Final leg drive is delayed until the arms and gravity have done their work.

22. Timing among three events—falling forward, arm swing, and leg drive. The arm swing is vigorous and contributes energy. Leg drive is powerful. Note (e) the legs are still coiled to strike. It takes patience. The arms and legs coordinate (f) for an effective forward drive.

21a

22a

21b

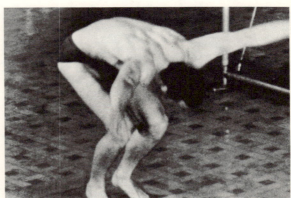

22b

21c

22c

22d

22e

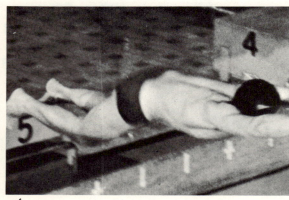

22f

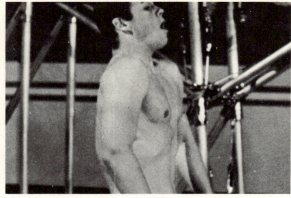

23

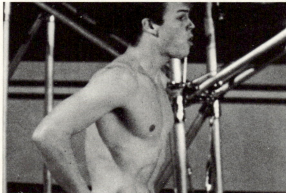

24

23. and **24.** Many swimmers take a series of deep breaths to hyperventilate just before the start.

25. Depth of the dive has to be right. Too deep a dive would lose time and momentum.

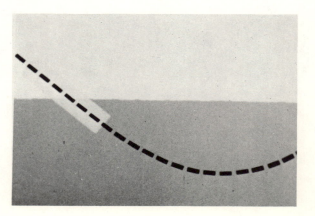

27. Initial speed of the glide is faster than swimming speed. Actual swimming should not start immediately. Wait until speed of glide slows down to swimming speed.

27a

27b

27c

26. Depth of the dive has to be right. A flat dive would dissipate energy.

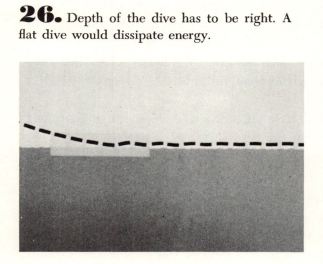

The Turn

The turn is a vital part of the race. It must be carried out well. The beginner may regard the turn as an obstacle and almost a nuisance. In contrast, the skilled swimmer sees the turn as an enormous advantage. He knows that the well-executed turn can increase speed and reduce over-all time. The records made in short pools are always faster than those made in long pools. That's because more turns are made in short pools.

The reason that the turn can add speed is that you have a chance to push from a solid surface, the wall of the pool. In addition, during the glide, a rest can be gained.

The task of the turn is to reverse direction and to do so quickly and efficiently. In freestyle swimming the rules no longer require a handtouch. Any part of the body can make contact with the pool wall. Hence for practical purposes there are no restrictions. You can turn almost any way that you want.

The fine sprinter uses some variation of the somersault turn. As he nears the wall, he dives, tucks, and twists. These actions put his legs in position to push against the wall. After the push, he glides and then resumes swimming.

To carry out the first part of the turn you've got to both somersault and twist. Let's consider the somersault. A good somersault really amounts to making an efficient change or transition. In normal swimming you are moving forward with your body level or in horizontal alignment. Your task becomes to destroy this stable, flat position and to spin quickly in the vertical plane.

The way to spin quickly is to create a force that pushes down your upper body and one that lifts your lower body. The movements that bring about these two results are as follows. If you drop your head, the water resistance or drag created by your upper body is greatly increased. The spinning action is started. At the same time you increase the speed of the somersault by creating an upward force on your lower body. You do this by driving downward with both your legs and your hands. The two forces, downward on the upper body and upward on the lower body, combine to speed up the somersault.

You also increase the speed of the somersault by flexing or tucking your body. By making your body compact it spins much easier and faster than if it were stretched out.

Twist. You can see that if you were to do only a somersault (actually, a half somersault), you would push off the wall while on your back. It takes a half twist of your body to put you on your stomach. As you are somersaulting you start twisting. This twisting action brings the legs slightly to one side. The feet leave the water. During the somersault, a quarter twist is enough. As a result of a quarter twist you will be on your side when you are ready to push off the wall. As you drive and start your glide, you make another quarter twist which puts you back in swimming position.

Timing. It's easy to know or recognize good timing of your turn. A well-timed turn will let you end up with your legs in a solid position against the wall. Your legs should have just the right amount of bend when they reach the wall. The optimum amount of leg bend will vary somewhat from swimmer to swimmer.

The key to good timing of the turn is the dive. If you start your dive too soon, you will have to wait and drift toward the pool wall, thus losing valuable time. If you dive too late, you will be cramped and won't have enough room for a good execution of your somersault and twist.

It takes practice and experience to develop reliable judgment as to when to start your dive. You have to work at it. Your judgment has to reach the point where you can start the dive quickly and decisively. Even the expert sometimes mistimes a turn. But even one bad turn can hurt him in a race against other champs. That's why he gives the turn a great deal of practice attention.

Off the wall. Your speed off the wall depends on two factors—the power of your leg drive and the streamlining of your body. You will want a powerful push off the wall. Pushing from a solid surface gives you a chance to develop great speed, and you will want to take full advantage of this opportunity. The leg drive should be an all-out effort.

As you push from the wall the arms are moved forward. The head is between the arms. During the glide the body is held straight. This streamling of the body reduces drag or resistance and thus helps to maintain speed.

As you drive off the wall and glide in a streamlined position, you have about the same situation as you have when you enter the water in the start. Because of the drive afforded by a solid surface, initial body speed is faster than swimming speed. You can see that if you try to swim too soon you will both reduce speed and waste energy. Patience is needed.

The more thoroughly that you understand the turn, the quicker you will master it. You will want to analyze each part of the turn—the dive, somersault, spin, twist, contact with the wall, push, streamlined position, glide, and when to resume swimming. But, of course, you will keep in mind that the parts must blend to make a turn that is decisive, smooth, continuous, and, above all, fast. After all, you are in a race. You can see that an effective turn is going to take understanding, work, and attention.

28a

28b

28c

29a

29b

29c

29d

28. The turn should never be viewed as a nuisance or obstacle. A well-executed turn actually increases swimming speed.

29. All fine sprinters use some form of the somersault turn. The start of the turn must be well timed but fast and decisive.

30c

30d

30. The somersaulting action has started (a and b). Photos c and d show the two main forces at work in spinning the body. The head lowers. The hands and legs push downward. The legs drive off the wall (g and h). The first part of the glide is on the side (i and j). Swimming starts (k) when the speed of the glide slows to swimming speed.

30a

30e

30b

30f

30g

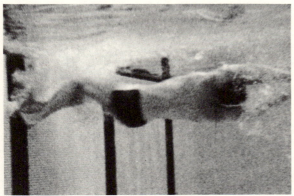

30h

30i

30j

30k

II. Butterfly Swimming

Introduction

The butterfly stroke, the newest of the racing strokes, has a short history. Its emergence as a separate competitive stroke goes back only to 1952. It all began in Brooklyn in 1933. A swimmer named Henry Meyer experimented with an above-water recovery of the arms in the breaststroke. He reasoned that recovery of the arms through the air instead of through the water would eliminate practically all resistance to arm action. Not only would the arms recover more quickly, but the reduction of drag would allow the body to move faster. As the breaststroke rules were then written, the above-water recovery did not seem to be in violation. When the new stroke was first used in competition, it naturally brought great astonishment along with strong protest. However, Meyer's innovation was ruled to be legal. A new method was born, and nearly all breaststrokers adopted it. In the 1952 Olympic Games all of the finalists used butterfly arm action.

To preserve the breaststroke, the governing body for international swimming made the butterfly a separate stroke, and the dolphin kick was legalized. The frog kick still remains legal, but it is not used by the top competitors.

Even though the butterfly is an offshoot of the breaststroke, the arm action and the kick of the butterfly are very much like those of the crawl. At first sight the butterfly stroke doesn't seem to be much like the crawl because in the butterfly both the arms and the legs work simultaneously, but if we trace the pattern of one arm, we can see that the butterfly arm action and the crawl arm action are similar. The butterfly kick and the crawl kick are also fundamentally alike. However, because of the involvement of the body and the up-and-down movement of the hips, the kick of the butterfly is fuller and probably more powerful than that of the crawl kick. Because of the similarities between the two strokes, the freestyler usually takes to the butterfly very readily.

Since the butterfly developed from the breaststroke, the rules for the two events are similar. There is the same insistence on symmetry and simultaneous action. The arms must move together both in recovery and during the arm pull. They must also move symmetrically, which means that in addition to moving together they must be at about the same height. Briefly put, one arm should be pretty much the mirror image of the other. The same holds true for the legs. The rules permit "simultaneous movements of the legs and feet in the vertical plane." Both the frog kick and the dolphin kick are allowed, and it is permissible to switch from one kick to the other during a race.

As in the breaststroke, "the body must be kept perfectly on the breast, and both shoulders in the horizontal plane." This rule should not present any problem, since its violation would offer no advantage.

You have to hold form in touching both at the turn and in finishing the race. "When touching at the turn or in finishing a race, the touch shall be made with both hands simultaneously on the same level. The shoulders shall be in a horizontal position in line with the surface of the water."

There has been a remarkable improvement in butterfly performance. Today the top fliers can defeat very good freestylers. Butterfly records are beginning to approach those for the freestyle. Many coaches and swimmers feel that the butterfly is still an unexploited stroke and that great further progress can be expected. Some even think that the butterfly will eventually prove faster than the crawl stroke. This could be, but at the present time it doesn't seem likely. The crawl has a mechanical advantage over the butterfly in that the crawl's alternate actions of both the arms and the legs provide a fairly even application of power. In contrast, in the butterfly, because the arms and legs have to work simultaneously, there is a tendency toward powerful surges followed by dead spots. The experts are working to minimize the dead spots—a difficult job to carry out within the framework of the present rules.

All strokes require strength, but the butterfly is surely the most strenuous of the strokes. Great upper-body strength is needed to carry out the form correctly, so the flier puts greater emphasis on special land exercises.

Body Position

When anything moves, its speed depends on propulsion and resistance. There are forces that create movement and those that tend to retard movement. So it is with swimming, regardless of the stroke used. If there were no resistance, a single stroke would move you indefinitely and at the same speed. Resistance cannot be entirely eliminated, but it can be reduced by maintaining a streamlined body position that keeps water drag to a minimum.

The butterfly is a spectacular stroke, and it tends to create the illusion of extreme up-and-down movement of the body, which can mislead the beginner. Careful observation of the great butterflier, however, shows that there is relatively little up-and-down movement. The upper body stays at about the same level during the entire stroke, and the shoulders remain near the surface. Because of the dolphin kick, the hips do have a slight vertical movement. The downbeat drives the hips upward, and the upbeat's reaction lowers the hips. Yet the up-and-down movement of the hips doesn't cover much of a range—only a few inches.

Most resistance is created by nonalignment. In moving through the water a body can be out of alignment along any of three axes. It can fail to be level, it can be sideways—that is, not in line with the direction of movement—or it can rotate along its long axis. The last two possible interferences with streamlining should not bother the butterflier, because the symmetrical and simultaneous movements of the stroke should insure against both rolling and lateral nonalignment. Hence, the flier is free to concentrate on keeping a level body position. The main task, then, is to keep the vertical movement of the body to a minimum. Any lowering of the body toward the vertical creates additional water resistance.

The biggest factor in stabilizing the body is the coordination between the action of the arms and the kick of the legs. Although the main function of the arms and legs is propulsive, their timing with each other is essential to efficient body position. Put briefly, the arms and legs can, with proper timing, counter each other's tendency to disturb body position. There will be a closer consideration of this timing in a later section.

The need to breathe always has some adverse effect on body position. At regular intervals the face has to be out of the water so that air can be taken in. In the butterfly stroke the interference with streamlining caused by breathing is minimized in two ways. First, the lifting of the head is timed with swimming action so that the breath is taken at a point when it least disturbs body position. Second, an effort is made to get the face out of the water without raising the upper body. This means that the neck muscles have to be used to lift the head.

Good body position can be described in fairly few words. This is particularly so in the case of the butterfly, because the streamlining problem exists with reference to only one aspect—keeping the body level. The description of good body position takes up only a small portion of this book, but that does not mean good body position is not important. Body position should always be emphasized. Keep in mind that even the most powerful arm pull and kick can be negated if the body position is not right.

1. The butterfly stroke is an undulating motion. The body plays an enormous part in propulsion, and at first glance it would seem that the flier is surging upward and downward. A careful look at these underwater photographs shows that up-and-down movement of the body does indeed exist but that it is not as extreme as it would appear—in fact, it can be measured in inches. The principle of keeping the best body position commensurate with effective propulsion is essential.

1a

1b

1c

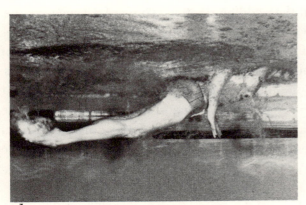

1d

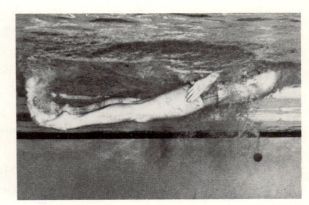

1e

1f

Arm Action

At first glance, the arm action of the butterfly seems strange and puzzling, especially if the view is from an underwater window. However, it can be clearly understood on a logical basis. Actually, the arm action in the butterfly is like that of the crawl. It's just that when both arms work together they trace a curious pattern.

As with all strokes, the butterfly arm action can be best understood in terms of what we might call the paddle principle. Think of a canoe paddle. The paddle is driven backward through the water and in this way supplies forward propulsion. The force of propulsion depends on a number of factors, but for practical purposes speed and direction are what matters. Propulsion depends on action and reaction. This is true of everything that moves, including jet planes. Action and reaction are always in opposite directions, so we know that we want the action of the arms to cause a backward drive in order best to drive the body forward. This, then, is the base from which we start. We can then consider modifications in technique to take account of other factors, such as body position.

If we are going to use the paddle analogy as a way of understanding arm action, we have to take account of the structure of the paddle. What directly and finally matters is the broad blade of the paddle, the part that drives below the surface of the water and moves relatively fast.

For the most part it is the hand that functions as the blade, although during some portion of the stroke the forearm can move fast enough to contribute to propulsion. The contribution of the upper arms and the other big muscles of the body is always indirect. Their job is to get the hands moving fast and in the right direction. Hence, strictly from the point of view of technique, our analysis of the arm stroke has to be concerned with what the hands are doing. Within such a framework let's take a look at the specifics of arm action.

The S pattern. Although there are slight variations, the general S pattern traced by hand is characteristic for all fine fliers. After the hands enter the water, the first movement is both outward and downward. The outward movement of the hands shifts smoothly to an inward movement. The hands come very close together at the point where they are directly under the shoulders. From then on, the hands move apart until the stroke is completed and the recovery begins.

The S pattern is a result of trying to make the arm stroke as efficient as possible throughout its entire length. The basic guiding principle is always action and reaction. We want the drive against the water to be as directly backward as possible. But we also have to take account of two other factors—body position and the ability to develop power. Perhaps a good way to understand the logic of the S pattern is to start with the idea that the arms could be kept straight and move directly backward in a vertical path during the full stroke. Then we can take a look at the modifications that are needed and the reasons for them.

When the hands enter the water, the arms are straight ahead in the direction in which the body is moving. Suppose the arms were kept straight and their first movement was directly downward. The downward action would produce an upward reaction, driving the body upward more than forward. There would be little contribution to forward speed, and there would be a loss of streamlining. Further, the arms would be in a poor mechanical position to exert power. The first part of such a stroke would therefore be clearly inefficient. However, efficiency would increase until the arms reached an up-and-down position. At this point the pull would be efficient—but only at this point. With the movement of the arms past the vertical position, the action would then become increasingly upward, forcing the body downward.

You can see that a straight-armed vertical pull cannot be truly efficient, because the action is directly backward at only one point. The goal of technique is to increase backward action over the entire arm stroke, and essential to reaching this goal is making use of the flexibility of the arms. By the appropriate bending of the arms the pull can be kept more backward, producing a greater forward reaction and thereby increasing the efficiency of the stroke.

Entry. As the arms finish their recovery, they are moving fast, and their speed should continue right into the water. Entry of the arms is almost straight ahead—they are just slightly to the outside. The palms are downward but turned enough so that the thumbs enter the water first. In this way the hands are in position to be blades for movement both outward and downward.

First part of the arm pull. As the outward-and-downward pull begins, the arms bend and the elbows are high. The bending of the arms and the raising of the elbows create a mechanical advantage, because the muscles quickly get into a favorable position to move the hands, which exert pressure against the water.

The hands come together. The hands reach their widest spread at about the time they are halfway to the downward vertical position. From there on, the hands start to come closer together, and the outward component gives way to an inward one. The elbows are kept high, while the hands rotate so that the palms face backward. As the hands come closer together, they can push more directly backward in alignment with the body. This is a highly efficient part of the stroke. At this point, because they are vertical, the forearms can also make a contribution to forward propulsion. The hands are closest together when the arms are directly beneath the body.

Past the vertical. After coming close together, the hands continue to sweep backward and outward. As the forearms lose their vertical position, they make less of a contribution to forward propulsion. The hands, however, continue to push the water directly backward. Flexion of the wrists permits the hands to be straight up and down almost to the very end of the stroke. The palms continue to act as efficient paddleblades. The outward, or rounded, action of the arms toward the finish of the stroke helps prepare for the recovery. If the arms were going straight back, they would have to stop to begin forward movement, but the rounded action allows the hands as they leave the water to maintain continuity of movement. The arms keep right on going.

Recovery. The final action of the arms in the water is really an anticipation of the recovery. Even before the hands leave the water, the arms are already starting to recover. No time is lost in making the recovery. The rounded action of the arms adds to momentum and ensures that the finish of the stroke blends smoothly into the recovery so that there is continuity of action.

The recovery is made above but close to the water. The hands literally skim over the water. Extra height of the hands would be wasteful of energy, and it would interfere with efficient form. Since there is no water resistance during the recovery, the arms can move fast and, at the same time, be relaxed. Power for the recovery comes from the muscles of the shoulders and upper back, and once the initial thrust has been made by these muscles, the arms can coast forward. When the hands leave the water, the palms are toward the rear. They rotate easily and smoothly during the recovery so that the fingers are pointing almost directly forward at entry. As the hands enter the water, it is important that the arms retain their momentum. Continuity of movement is essential both to body position and the efficiency of the stroke.

Breathing. The movement required for breathing is bound to interfere with streamlining. The goal is to keep this interference to a minimum while, of course, still taking in an adequate amount of air. To inhale air the face has to be lifted partially out of the water. The best technique is to lift the head without lifting the entire upper body. The neck is stretched backward so that most of the face is above the water. At this point, the eyes are looking straight ahead and the head is brought no higher than necessary, the chin remaining in the water. The beginner may have to lift his head a little higher to avoid taking in water, but with experience he will learn to keep his head fairly low and still avoid the intake of water.

The best time to lift the head is when the shoulders are highest, and even with an efficient arm stroke its early action causes some lifting of the upper body. The upward reaction of the arm action is completed at about the time that the arms reach the vertical. This is the most favorable point for the head to rise so that a breath can be taken. Inhalation is fast so that the head can quickly return to swimming position, and the breath is held to increase buoyancy. Exhalation occurs just before the next inhalation. Frequency of breathing, as in the crawl stroke, is usually determined by the length of the race. In most races breathing is carried out every two or three strokes. But some swimmers breathe every stroke. Apparently the breathing pattern is an individual matter, each swimmer finding the pattern that suits him best.

2. The powerful butterfly arm pull traces an S pattern.

2a

2d

2e

2h

3. Because the butterfly stroke is continuous and rhythmic, the arm pull blends into the recovery. The arms finish their drive and skim forward close to the surface of the water. With no water resistance during the recovery, the arms have a good chance to relax. The powerful muscles of the trunk supply the impetus (d). After the intake of air has been completed, the head is again in the water to aid streamlining.

3a

2b

2c

2f

2g

3b

3c

3d

3e

4. Breathing is co-ordinated with the arm
action. To preserve good body position the
neck muscles are used to raise the face out
of the water. The intake of air is carried out
quickly and the face is again lowered.

4a

4b

The Dolphin Kick

The legs are a powerful part of the body. They are at least twice as strong as the arms, and they have much greater endurance. You can move around all day on your legs—and for only a matter of seconds on your arms. Runners depend entirely on their legs for propulsion; the arms have only a balancing effect. In swimming, however, the arms are the main source of propulsion, and the legs are used primarily for balance.

Because the legs represent such an enormous potential source of power, swimming experts have always been frustrated by their inability to make better use of them. The dolphin kick—which, as indicated by its name, is meant to simulate the powerful swimming action of the dolphin—may represent a partial solution.

The mechanics of running are not entirely simple, but compared to swimming they are relatively easy to grasp. In running only the feet are in contact with the medium. All effort is intended to build up the speed of the feet against the ground. A much more complicated situation exists in swimming, and although we don't have to be too concerned with the complications, it is helpful to note a few of them. The most obvious one is that both the hands and the feet are propelling surfaces. Another is that the forearms and forelegs, during parts of their action, also become propelling surfaces. Of course, there is an enormous complication in that, unlike the runner, who moves on the surface, the swimmer is moving *through* the water. That means that the swimmer has to pay as much attention to the water resistance he creates as he does to the propulsive power he develops. Kicking, then, is not the simple act it may at first appear to be. It is realistic and helpful to mention the complications that exist, because their analysis will contribute to more effective technique, but for our purposes now it is enough to remember that the arms are the primary source of propulsion.

In swimming there are two main sources of propulsion for moving the same body—the arms and the legs. Each can work alone to move the body forward, but combining their actions may or may not increase forward speed. It is clear enough that the arms are the primary source of speed, so we must see in what ways the kick can increase the speed that arm action alone can build up. To put it briefly, the legs must operate in such a way that they get the feet moving backward faster than the body is moving forward. That may sound a little complicated, but let's take a further look. If the arms alone can generate a forward body speed of four miles per hour, the kick can make a contribution to propulsion only when the feet are moving backward faster than four miles per hour. Of course, the faster the better. Anything less than four miles per hour would create drag, or water resistance.

In addition to foot speed there are other factors in assessing the efficiency of the kick. The kick has to be made in such a way as to keep water resistance low. The legs could produce propulsive foot speed and, at the same time, nullify the gain by also producing excessive drag. The kick has still another important function. It helps to stabilize body position and thus contributes to streamlining.

A look at the dolphin kick. The dolphin kick is very likely the most powerful of all the swimming kicks. The entire body seems to contribute to the power of the drive, as the body and legs perform like a whip in building up great velocity of the feet. Unlike other strokes where hip position is fixed, the hips move up and down in the dolphin kick. This hip mobility is a significant feature in developing power.

Because the arms pull together rather than alternately, there is no roll of the body. The kicking action is straight up and down. There is no diagonal component as in the kicking action for the crawl or backstroke because there is no need to compensate for or adjust to a body roll.

Just as the arm action of the butterfly is similar to that of the crawl stroke, the kicks of the two strokes have the same basic features. Of course, there is the obvious difference that in the dolphin kick both legs move together, not alternately. The dolphin kick is fuller and more powerful, the increased range of the kick coming about through hip mobility.

When carried out well, the dolphin kick is smooth, undulating, and continuous. It does indeed resemble the graceful swimming of the dolphin. Even though the dolphin kick should be a continuous action, it is useful for the purposes of analysis to break it down into two parts—the upbeat and the downbeat.

Upbeat. The upbeat has to be viewed primarily as a preparation for the powerful downbeat. Most experienced coaches believe that the upbeat can make no direct contribution to forward propulsion, but that it has two alternate functions. First, it prepares for the downbeat. Second, the reaction of the upbeat helps to stabilize body position. The argument is that since the upbeat can make no contribution to body speed, the main concentration should be on raising the legs with a minimum of water resistance. In brief, the upbeat cannot help propel the body forward, but it should not hinder by creating unnecessary drag.

Actually, there is some evidence that the upbeat can make a contribution to forward speed. Definitive studies are difficult to come by, and the matter may remain in doubt for some time to come. However, the test of contribution to propulsion is basically simple. As we have stated, if you can get the feet moving backward faster than the body is moving forward, there is a contribution to speed. Slow-motion movies of some fine swimmers suggest that this can be done. Among the top performers, especially those with good ankle flexibility, water pressure during the upbeat bends the ankle so that the sole of the foot is facing backward, which could not happen unless the legs were contributing to forward speed. Without such a contribution the ankles would flex in the opposite direction so that the toes would point backward. In any case, the upbeat should be carried out with the intention of making a contribution to forward speed.

At the end of the downbeat the hips are high and the legs are straight. This position comes about naturally as a result of the downbeat. The legs are kept straight as they start upward. It's important that there be no bend at the knees, because a bend would cause drag. Some loose-jointed swimmers can even gain from hyperextension, a "reverse bend" at the knees. The ankles flex so that the soles of the feet are facing backward. This position of the feet allows the important backward push against the water. The upbeat ends when the legs are about parallel to the surface of the water.

Downbeat. The downward movement of the legs is the obvious source of power. In whipping downward the legs build up to a fast and powerful backward thrust of the feet. The speed of the downbeat can be so great that even the forelegs contribute to propulsion. The power of the downbeat is due to the construction of the legs. The legs can straighten with great power; the extensor muscles of the thighs are capable of enormous drive.

At the finish of the upbeat, the legs are still straight. Because of the reaction created by the upward movement of the legs, the hips are at their highest point. The downbeat is begun by a downward movement of the upper legs. The lower legs continue their upward movement, rising almost to the surface. This combination of actions causes the knees to bend, and at the point of fullest bend the upper leg and foreleg form approximately a right angle. After maximum leg bend has been reached, the forelegs start downward. At the same time, the upper legs continue their downward drive. The whip is ready to be cracked. The lower legs, already moving fast, now receive terrific momentum from the straightening of the legs.

Ankle flexibility is vital. Although the forelegs can and should contribute to forward propulsion, the feet are the main blades. It's not enough for the feet to be moving fast; they must be positioned to push the water backward. A different part of the foot is used for the downbeat. Remember that during the upbeat it is the soles of the feet that are driven backward. During the downbeat it is the insteps, or tops of the feet, that are the pushing surfaces. This calls for an extreme change of foot position. Looseness or flexibility of the ankles is the key, because if the ankles are loose enough, water pressure positions the feet correctly.

The more direct is the backward drive, the greater is the contribution to forward propulsion. But there is always a downward action, and the reaction raises the hips to the surface. The legs are fully extended at the end of the downbeat, and you are ready to begin the upbeat. The action is continuous and flowing, with the downbeat blending into the upbeat and, in turn, the upbeat blending into the downbeat.

5. As a result of the dolphin kick, the hips move up and down. This movement is a natural reaction to the kicking motion and also makes the kick more powerful. The up-and-down movement is not as extreme as it appears. Check the pool line in the background for an idea of the range of hip movement.

5a

5b

5c

5d

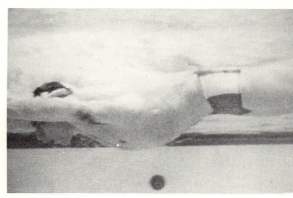

5e

6. It's velocity and positioning of the feet that count. The feet must not only be moving fast; they must be pointed in the right direction so that the push is backward. The feet will tend to push the water backward if the ankles are loose.

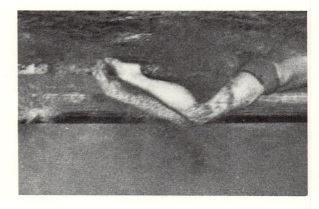

7. The downbeat of the dolphin kick is a powerful smash that should build up great velocity of the feet. Although the upbeat may make some contribution to propulsion, it is primarily a preparation for the downbeat. The goal is to develop a whiplike action of the body and legs that results in the feet moving fast.

7a

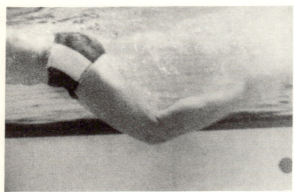

7d

7e

7h

8. The dolphin kick—here somewhat exaggerated by use of the kickboard—represents a powerful build-up of energy which propels the body forward. In (b) the propelling power of the feet is clearly seen.

8a

7b

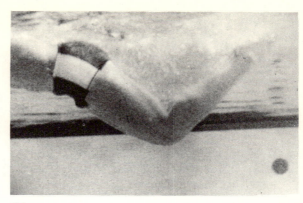

7c

7f

7g

8b

8c

Coordinating the Arms and Legs

In timing arm action with the kick there are two primary goals: reducing "dead spots" in propulsion and maintaining good body position. In the four competitive strokes the ratio of arm pulls to leg kicks varies over a considerable range. For the breaststroke the ratio is one to one. That is, for each arm pull there is one kick. For the crawl and backstroke the ratio is one to six, or one arm pull to six beats of the legs. In the butterfly there is one simultaneous pull of the arms for every two kicks. There is nothing magical or forever fixed about the ratio of any of the four strokes. Experimentation continues as coaches and swimmers look for more effective techniques, and we may see some changes, especially in the crawl and backstroke. However, in the case of the butterfly the ratio of one arm pull to two kicks seems likely to remain unchanged. There are compelling reasons for this ratio.

Let's look at the timing between the arms and the legs in the butterfly and the reasons for it. A useful starting place is at the point of full recovery as the arms are just entering the water. Because the arms have been recovering rather than driving, there is a tendency for the body to lose speed—to hit a "dead spot." This relative slowing down presents a good opportunity for the kick to be effective. Remember that the effectiveness of the kick depends on driving the feet backward faster than the body is moving forward, so the kick is most effective at the body's slowest speed. The downbeat of the legs begins just as the arm pull begins.

In addition to taking advantage of the relative slowdown of the body, the kick helps to stabilize the body. Even with ideal form the pull of the arms cannot be entirely backward. There is always some forward component to the pull. The downward action of the pull produces an upward reaction which tends to lift the upper body. A lifting of the upper body would drop the lower body, and the resulting position would increase water resistance. But the downward thrust of the legs lifts the hips, counteracting the tendency for the hips to drop. The total result is that the body tends to remain level, and a streamlined position is maintained.

The second downbeat of the legs takes place during the last portion of the arm stroke. At this point, the body is moving at its fastest, and the kick has less chance to contribute to forward propulsion. You will recall the basic principle that in order to contribute to forward speed the pushing area must move backward faster than the body is moving forward. Obviously, the faster the body is moving the more difficult it is to meet this requirement. Hence, the second kick cannot contribute as much to forward propulsion as the first kick does.

The important function of the second downbeat of the legs is to help maintain body stability, to counteract the effects produced by the last part of the arm action. As the hands and forearms reach the vertical, the arm stroke is at its most efficient because the water is being pushed almost directly backward, but past the vertical point both the hands and the forearms are moving upward as well as backward. This upward action produces a downward reaction, which tends to lower the hips. Were it not for the neutralizing effect of the kick, the hips would drop, and there would be increased drag or water resistance. At this critical point the downbeat causes an upward reaction. With proper timing the reactions produced by the arms and legs cancel each other, and the body tends to remain in a streamlined position.

In summary, then, the two-beat kick of the butterfly serves two important purposes—propulsion and streamlining of the body. In attaining these goals timing is important. The first kick comes when it can contribute maximum propulsion and also help maintain good body position. The second kick contributes less to movement, because the downbeat is made when the body is moving at its greatest speed, but it is important to preserve streamlining.

9. In this sequence the double function of the dolphin kick is seen. As the arms are recovering and the body is slowing down (c, d, and e), the kick has its best chance to be effective. Another kick compensates for the lifting of the body by the arms (f, g, and h).

9*a*

9*d*

9*e*

9*h*

10. This sequence demonstrates the ability of the dolphin kick to stabilize the body as well as provide power. The second kick per arm cycle, shown here, is the one that counteracts the downward reaction of the arm pull and so helps to keep the body level.

10*c*

10*d*

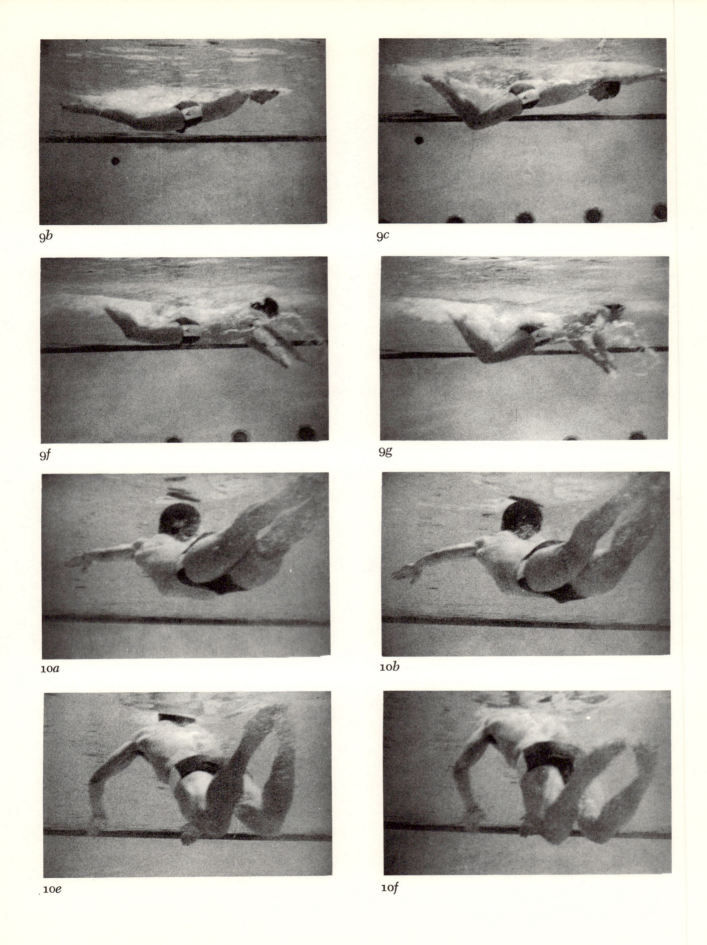

9b

9c

9f

9g

10a

10b

10e

10f

10g

10h

10i

10j

11. As the arms are partly through the powerful pull, the legs, seen here from the rear, are positioning for the strong blow that will both maintain body position and contribute to forward propulsion.

11a

11b

11c

The Start

The butterfly start is the same as that used in the crawl stroke, and, except for the angle of entry into the water, it is also similar to that of the breast-stroke. Before turning to the butterfly, most swimmers begin with either the crawl stroke or the breaststroke, or both. Hence, all the practice effort in starting for these two strokes has carry-over value for the butterfly start.

You may already be familiar with the techniques of starting, which are not difficult to understand. What matters most are the practice time and effort given to them. Most fine swimmers are now thoroughly convinced that the start is a vital part of a race and are willing to give the start the practice attention it deserves.

Unfortunately, even now some experts take the position that somehow the start will automatically work itself out, that a reasonably good start will come about without direct attention. It may be true that a fairly good start can be worked out without intensive attention to detail, but a fairly good start isn't enough in an era when place winners are so close at the finish line that they often have to be separated by electronic devices.

Making the most of a solid surface. Man can move about five times faster on land than he can through the water. That's because he can create a greater reaction driving against a solid surface than he can by driving against liquid. The swimmer has the opportunity to use a solid surface only at the start and during the turns, and both opportunities should be thoroughly exploited. Our present concern is with the start.

The goals of the start. Realistic measures of a start's effectiveness are speed and distance. You want to get out fast and far. In practice starts against teammates and in actual competition you will get a good idea of where you stand. If you're behind when you surface, you know that a lot has to be done. If you are even, that's not good enough. If you are ahead, it's encouraging that you have an edge—but the job is to work to make the edge even greater. Another way to evaluate your performance is to have your speed checked by a stopwatch.

The start should be a smooth co-ordinated act. One part blends into and influences the next part. Basically, there are four goals of the start. First, it's important to react quickly to the gun. Second, you want to develop power off the blocks for speed and distance. Third, you want to enter the water in as knifelike a manner as possible so that there is minimum resistance. Fourth, once in the water, you should maintain a streamlined position of the body to take advantage of the speed you have generated.

"Take your mark." At the starter's command you move easily into place. The rules require only that you hold a steady position. Feet are spaced comfortably, between six and twelve inches apart. The toes grip the edge of the starting platform to afford a firmer base for the drive. There is a slight bend to the knees, and body weight is balanced over the balls of the feet. The body is bent forward, and the arms hang loosely. It is important to be relaxed, yet at the same time to concentrate on movement. A great body of experimental literature demonstrates that reaction time is faster when attention is on the move to be made rather than on the stimulus.

When the gun sounds. With enough practice and with concentration on movement, the sound of the gun puts you into action. The body moves forward, and at the same time the arms, kept fairly straight, begin their circular swing. In this way the arms develop greater momentum and are co-ordinated better with the body's downward and forward movement. During the first part of their swing, the arms are wide, but as they descend, they move close to the body. They continue their vigorous swing until just before they become parallel to the surface of the water. At this point arm movement is stopped, and the momentum of the arms is transferred to the body.

The legs increase their bend, the increased flexion at the knees serving two important purposes. The bend helps to lower the body, and it allows the legs to be better prepared for a powerful drive off the platform. The knees reach their maximum bend at about the time that the arms are swinging past the legs on their way forward. From this point on, the legs begin to straighten while keeping contact with the platform. The legs continue their drive, and the body continues to lower as it straightens. When the leg drive is completed and contact with the platform is broken, the body is extended and almost parallel to the water's surface. The arms are forward.

Entry. An efficient entry preserves the speed that has been generated off the starting platform. This means creating the least possible resistance upon entering the water. The body literally forms a straight line from outstretched hands to outstretched toes, with the head between the arms. The hands enter the water first. Body position is held. This is one of the rare times when relaxation is not useful. The body must be held rather stiffly so that its streamlining is not disturbed.

The angle of entry is now obviously important, but not so long ago, when it was thought that the body should land completely flat or parallel to the water, swimmers used the so-called racing start. There was a great splash, with the arms "contributing" by vigorously slapping the water. The unfortunate idea was to avoid sinking in the water, there being a peculiar illusion that the swimmer could remain on the surface after the start. Further, it was believed that he could and should start swimming immediately. Observation and experience have made it absolutely clear that a completely flat dive causes loss of body speed and is otherwise harmful. All coaches now recognize that the start should bring you underwater. It is possible, however, to dive too deeply, and in such a case valuable time is lost in getting back to the surface. It takes practice and experience to get a feel for the right angle of entry.

In the water. No matter what the stroke, the start, because it is made against a solid surface, always develops speed that is greater than swimming speed. The logic of making the best use of a glide that is faster than swimming speed is compelling. It's easy to see that a premature effort to swim not only slows you down but also takes away the valuable relaxation that the glide should provide. This principle is easy enough to grasp but is usually difficult to put into practice. Patience and poise are the critical factors. Particularly among beginners, there is a strong tendency under the excitement of competition to try to start swimming immediately, but training and experience produce the poise that lets you follow the basic principle: swimming starts only when the speed of the glide slows down to swimming speed.

It is possible to start swimming too late, but this is an unusual error, and when it does occur, it results from too steep an entry, so that glide speed becomes less than swimming speed before the surface is reached. Too much depth can be partially corrected by positioning the arms and head to guide the body upward.

Future starting techniques. Except for the backstroke, starting rules are not very restricting, the basic requirement being that the swimmer "hold a steady balance for an appreciable length of time." That gives the swimmer a lot of leeway in taking a starting position, so changes in starting technique may be seen in the future.

Considerable attention is being given to the "grab" start, which a number of swimmers are using in top-level competition. It follows the lead offered by sprinters in track a few generations ago. In the grab start the arms, instead of simply hanging downward, are lowered so that the hands can grasp the underside of the starting platform. The head is low, so that the line of vision is almost directly downward.

This start is intended to increase the amount of crouch, lowering the body's center of gravity and thus shortening the interval between the sound of the gun and the final leg drive. The leg drive can be efficient only when the body is low enough for the major thrust to be forward rather than upward. The idea is that the grab start immediately places the body in the lowered position. There is no waiting for gravity to do the job. Surely the idea has merit. However, the grab start does not lower the body's center of gravity all that much. At the present time the future of the grab start is still in doubt, but this new method is worth watching.

Improvements in starting technique may not arrive in a dramatic or radical way. There may be a series of gradual refinements, each making the start slightly more efficient. However, they can add up to a significant result.

12. The start of the butterfly is the same as that used in freestyle swimming. The basic goals are to get away fast, develop power, and enter the water in a streamlined position.

12a

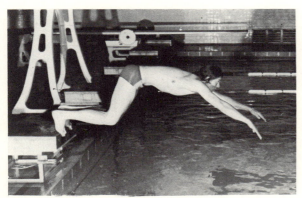

12b

12c

12d

12e

12f

13. While the body is falling toward efficient driving position, the circular and vigorous action of the arms develops power. The arms continue to swing until they are in line with the body. They then stop, and their energy is transferred to the body to increase forward movement.

13*a*

13*d*

13*e*

14. Great interest is now being shown in the grab start. It is thought that an advantage can be gained by having the body's center of gravity lower when the gun sounds. A disadvantage may be the lessened arm action, and more experience with this start is needed. All ambitious swimmers, however, will want to follow the findings concerning the effectiveness of this new technique.

14*a*

13b

13c

13f

14b

14c

The Turn

A turn represents a great opportunity for increased speed. Of course, this opportunity is open to all competitors, so it's best to assume that your opponents are also going to try to make the most of the opportunity the turn presents. That means your turn has to be efficient so that you don't give away any advantage. Better yet, make it your goal to polish your turn so that you gain an advantage.

The tests of a good turn are two. First, is the turn made within the rules? Second, is the turn as fast as possible?

Rules. What the rules really amount to is that you must be swimming butterfly form when you touch the wall and return to butterfly form before you lose contact with the wall. Specifically, the rules state:

> When touching at the turn or in finishing a race, the touch shall be made with both hands simultaneously on the same level, and with the shoulders in the horizontal plane. Once a legal touch has been made, the contestant may turn in any manner desired, but the prescribed form must be attained before the feet leave the wall in the push-off.

> When a contestant is in the underwater position after the start, when turning, or during the race, he is allowed to make one or more kicks.

Disqualification, of course, means loss of the race. Even if you have a large lead and are doing everything else well, all is in vain if you are disqualified.

The feeling is even worse if you disqualify your relay team. Hence the need to be aware of the rules at all times when you are practicing the turn. A good policy is to try never to make a practice turn that violates the rules, so there will be no probability of disqualification. In this way you will be freer to concentrate on technique and speed.

Speed. Obviously you want the turn to be as fast as possible, but the significant speed is not simply that of the body's changing direction. Both the speed of the approach and the speed off the wall are essential. To get a realistic measure of the speed of your turn, we would have to select a spot perhaps some ten yards or so from the wall and then time you from the time you pass this spot on your way to the wall until you pass it again on your return from the wall. The time would reflect the efficiencies of the major components of the turn: the approach, the pivot at the wall, and the drive off the wall.

Nearing the wall. An efficient approach to the wall calls for good timing. Ideally, the arms should be extended and ready to make the touch. This means that you should be at the wall just as the arms are completing the recovery, at which point they are extended forward. The obvious errors in timing are nearing the wall during the arm pull or getting there too long after the arms have recovered. In the first case, by the time the arms can recover and extend you can literally be jammed against the wall and unable to operate efficiently. In the other case, you have already recovered, and you have to wait for the body's momentum to bring your hands to the wall. When this happens, there is an obvious loss of speed.

The solution to the problem of timing lies in practice. Through countless practice turns you can develop a "feel" that brings you to the wall at the right time. You learn almost unconsciously and instinctively to make slight adjustments during the last several strokes. The lifting of the head during air intake lets you perceive the distance to the wall.

At the wall. The rules are of prime importance. Both hands must touch the wall together and at the same level. The shoulders must be horizontal when the touch is made. After you satisfy the rules, you can turn any way you want to. You just have to back in a correct position before you leave the wall. The rules for the turn are similar to those for the breaststroke, and so is the technique of turning.

Upon making contact with the wall there are two basic jobs for the arms to do—push and lift. The pushing task is the more important of the two. The lifting movement is made easier if there is a gutter to be grasped. Lacking a gutter, the deck of the pool can be used if it is low enough. In some pools there may be only the wall to work with.

When the hands reach the wall, the bend of the arms is partial. They have a slight "give." One arm does the work against the wall, while the other contributes to the turn by whipping around toward the opposite end of the pool. Which hand works against the wall and which hand whips is, of course, determined by whether you want to turn to the right or to the left. The direction selected is a matter of personal preference, but for ease of description let's assume you are turning to the right. Upon contact the arms push down to lift the upper body. The lifting movement of the right arm is very brief, because the right arm quickly leaves the wall to begin its whipping action.

When the touch is made, the legs begin to tuck under to make the body more compact. The turning radius is reduced, and the body is able to turn faster and more easily. The legs maintain their flexed position until the feet are placed solidly against the wall.

While the legs are doing their jobs of tucking and positioning themselves against the wall, the arms continue to work, with one arm pushing and the other whipping about. Once the arms have completed their contribution to the turning movements, their goal is to attain position for effective streamlining of the body. The arms move forward so that the head is between them. In the final position the arms are straight and parallel to the surface of the water with the hands close together.

During the turn the lifting action of the arms brings the head out of the water—but just out of the water, not much more. An effective rule is to lift the body just enough so that a breath can be taken in. It's easy to see that extra lifting wastes energy and also interferes with carrying out correct technique.

The tests for a good turn, then, are legality and efficiency. The two points of possible disqualification are at the touch and upon leaving the wall. Using the turning technique described in this section, you should have no problem in staying within the rules. It will come to your attention that some outstanding swimmers have been experimenting with a riskier type of turning method. The fastest kind of turn is, of course, the somersault turn used in freestyle swimming, because for all practical purposes there are no restrictions on the freestyle turn. There doesn't even have to be a hand touch. It's natural enough for fliers to eye the freestyle turn with the hope that they can make use of its features and still not risk disqualification. It doesn't seem useful, at this point, to get involved in a full description of the flip or somersault turn, but we can mention the major difficulty in carrying out such a turn while staying within the rules for the butterfly stroke. In making the somersault turn, because there is really only a half somersault, there has to be a rotation of the body. It's very hard to squeeze in this rotation between the two points of wall touch and departure from the wall. There is a natural tendency to start the rotation before the touch— which calls for disqualification. And there is a similar natural tendency to complete the rotation of the body after breaking contact with the wall— which also calls for disqualification. In summary, the turn used by the great majority of fliers presents very little problem of disqualification. The experimental turns are risky, but they should be watched.

The other and obvious test of the turn is its speed. But, as mentioned earlier, any measure of speed should reflect the overall picture, including the speed of approach to the wall. That's why the speed of the turn should be timed from a selected point considerably away from the wall, ten yards or so.

All aspects of the turn deserve attention. However, a significant check-point occurs as the body is ready to drive off the wall. The body should, of course, be fully turned and in the new direction of swimming. The legs should be flexed, with the feet in solid contact with the wall. The arms are forward to aid in streamlining. Reaching an effective push-off suggests that the turn is being carried out at least reasonably well.

Off the wall. The leg drive off the wall should be as full and as powerful as possible. The use of a solid surface to push against presents the opportunity to generate great speed, and for this reason an attempt to swim immediately would produce water resistance. It's important to remember that initial glide speed should be greater than swimming speed. Hence, after the push off the wall, the first job is to hold a streamlined position. Swimming starts only when the glide speed slows to swimming speed. Some swimmers prefer to start with the kick alone, while others begin with leg and arm action together.

Similarity to the breaststroke turn. The butterfly rules are the same as those for the breaststroke, and the techniques for the two turns are similar. The main differences are timing and depth in the water. The timing of the butterfly turn is faster, because you are approaching the wall at greater speed, and the legs are in a better position for a quicker tuck. The butterfly turn is shallower than the breaststroke turn. In leaving the wall the breaststroke swimmer needs greater depth to take advantage of the rules. The butterfly swimmer doesn't require this depth.

15. These are the basic features of the turn: The wall is approached at full speed (a). Timing is important and comes from practice. The hands touch the wall together and at the same level according to the rules (b). The body tucks to make the turn faster and easier (c). Leg drive determines the speed off the wall (d and e). The streamlined position is resumed (f), and the speed generated by the drive of the legs is held patiently until the body slows to swimming speed (g).

15a

15d

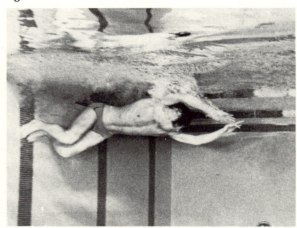

15e

15*b*

15*c*

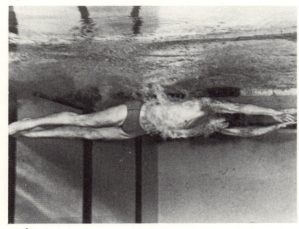

15*f*

15*g*

16. A full action sequence of the turn shows the essentials in detail. The first requirement is that the touch satisfy the rules (a). The wall is approached at full speed, and the turning action starts immediately (b). A fast turn depends on both the arm action and the tucking of the body (c, d, and e). The legs reach a power position against the wall (f), and the drive of the legs generates great speed (g, h, and i). Back to correct position (j), streamlining is held to maintain speed (k, l, and m) until the start of swimming (n).

16*a*

16*d*

16*e*

16*h*

16*i*

16*l*

16*m*

16b

16c

16f

16g

16j

16k

16n

17. The pushing hand completes a powerful drive off the wall and then whips around to a forward position.

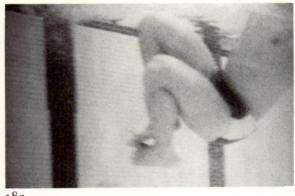

17a

17d

18. Leg placement is critical in an effective turn. The feet are placed solidly against the wall with the legs bent.

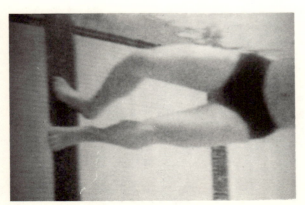

18a

18d

17b

17c

18b

18c

III. Backstroke Swimming

Introduction

Like most other athletic activities, swimming has deep roots in antiquity. The few bold ancients who braved the streams, lakes, and even the sea itself probably tried a great variety of propulsive methods. They may have felt more comfortable on their backs because of the ease of breathing in that form of swimming.

There is a great attraction in swimming on your back. If you look around any public pool, you will see people of all shapes and sizes paddling about on their backs. What they are really doing is assuming the basic floating position and propelling themselves by any method that may occur to them.

When competitive swimming first became popular, there were no stroke classes. In a race you could swim any way you wanted to. The backstroke, enjoyable as it was, wasn't used in competition, simply because it was not as fast as the other strokes. The backstroke emerged as a competitive stroke only when it was established as a separate class in the early part of this century.

Modern backstroke technique is the product of much trial and error and the constructive thinking of numerous coaches and athletes. Many methods of pulling and kicking have been used over the years. Any method could be tried, because the rules presented very few restrictions. To stay within the rules all you had to do was to stay on your back. By gradual evolution of technique the backstroke has become somewhat similar to the crawl stroke—except, of course, upside down.

Approach. In our efforts to understand the backstroke, it is best to start with a simple and clear approach. All sports activities accumulate superstitions and unsupported opinions about how to do things. These views can make athletic life complicated. Our criteria for technique are simple. Anything moving through the water has its speed determined by two factors: propulsion and resistance. When we examine technique, then, we are concerned only with what makes for more effective propulsion and what reduces water resistance, or drag. Everything else is irrelevant.

As technique has progressed, so have training methods. The present-day swimmer is stronger and much better conditioned than were his predecessors. Excellent technique, important as it is, is not enough. The swimmer needs to draw upon the best methods available to build strength and endurance.

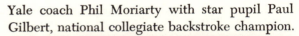

Yale coach Phil Moriarty with star pupil Paul Gilbert, national collegiate backstroke champion.

Body Position

Correct body position is critical to swimming, for two reasons. First, body position determines the amount of water resistance, or drag. Second, body position affects propulsion. In the backstroke body position is particularly important to the efficiency of the kick.

As a backstroker, you share a common problem with anyone who wants to move fast or with anything that is intended to move fast. Resistance has to be kept down as much as possible. When there is a constant amount of propulsive force, speed becomes strictly a matter of how much you can reduce resistance. That's why it is important to give a lot of attention to positioning your body so that there is the least amount of water drag.

No matter what the stroke, all swimmers face a somewhat similar task in reducing water resistance. The details vary from stroke to stroke, but the basic approach is the same. For every stroke the position of least resistance to the water is one in which the body is flat or parallel to the water's surface and in alignment with the direction in which the body is going. If we were concerned only with attaining a streamlined position, there would be little or no problem. The basic problem arises because parts of the body, the arms and legs, have to be used for propulsion. Also, of course, breathing has to be considered. So we have to compromise. "Ideal" body position has to be changed somewhat to take account of arm action, leg action, and breathing.

Let's start with an ideal streamlined position and then see what changes have to be made. If streamlining were the only consideration, your body would be parallel to the surface of the water. That means that your feet would also be close to the surface. But to kick effectively, your feet have to be deeper in the water. Thus, you can't remain perfectly flat. You have to be slanting downward along the long axis of your body from your head to your feet.

A perfectly flat position would also present a breathing problem. With your head back in the water and your vision directed straight upward, movement through the water would cause the water to rush over your face. Efficient breathing would then be impossible.

The problems of getting the legs to the right depth and of efficient breathing can be solved together by the correct positioning of the head. The head is bent forward so that the chin touches or almost touches the chest. Vision is directed backward so that you are looking just slightly above your toes. Head position is comfortable and without tension. Your nose and mouth are both clear of the water. There is then no obstacle to breathing. In all other competitive strokes the intake of air has to be carefully timed with either the turning or lifting of the head, and head movement has to be coordinated with movement of the limbs. Not so in the backstroke. In normal backstroke swimming you are free to breathe any time and in any rhythm that suits you.

As in most athletic activities, the head is an important controlling factor. Body position is very sensitive to the movement and positioning of the head. Once a good position has been assumed, it's important that the head stay put. Movement of the head, up and down or back and forth, would interfere with efficient body position.

The incline of the body is further aided by correct arm action. As the arm enters the water, there is a downward press. From this downward action there is an upward reaction. The upper body is raised.

The raising of the upper body depresses the lower body. The legs can be comfortably placed deep enough to do their job of kicking. But the lowering of the legs should never be gained at the expense of increased water resistance. This means avoiding the common tendency to lower the legs by simply sitting down in the water or letting the hips sag. You can easily see the great drag that this lowering of the hips would create. To counteract this tendency many fine backstrokers make a special effort to arch their backs. In this way the hips are prevented from dropping, and the body tends to remain straight.

So far, we've been talking about body position with reference to one axis. This is the position that one observes from a side or profile view. Along this one axis the tests for effective body position are: (1) Is the face clear of the water? (2) Are the legs deep enough to kick without breaking the surface? (3) Does the body form a straight line? As a practical matter, body position along this axis is the most important and should get the most practice attention. However, body position does have to be considered along the two other axes.

The body moves faster if it can stay in alignment with the direction in which it is going. Visualize a straight line along your lane in the pool. The goal is to keep your body right along this line and not let it swerve back and forth. For the most part arm and leg action control this alignment. The more arm action is directed backward rather than laterally, the more the body tends to move in a straight line. Also, leg action can compensate for the tendency of the body to get out of alignment.

Strictly from the standpoint of water resistance, it would be best if the body did not rotate around its long axis. A stable body would pose less resistance. But a certain amount of rotation is necessary for the arms to get their work done, for an effective arm pull. But rotation should be only for the sake of a more effective arm pull. The fine backstroker rotates as much as he has to—and only that much.

To summarize body position, you want your body to be as streamlined as possible. The more you can cut down on drag, the faster you will go. Even enormous power can be negated by water resistance. It pays for you and your coach to make constant checks on body position.

1. Good body position is essential to speed, but streamlining has to be a compromise. The legs have to be low enough in the water to kick efficiently. At the same time, the body is kept in alignment. Sagging at the hips should be avoided. Although the body has to rotate to add power to the arm pull (*e*, *f*, and *g*), this departure from streamlined position is kept to a minimum.

1*a*

1*d*

1*e*

2. Head position is critical to good body position. The inclined position of the head tends to control the angle and depth of the body. In addition, the inclined head acts as the prow of a ship in cutting through the water.

2*a*

2*d*

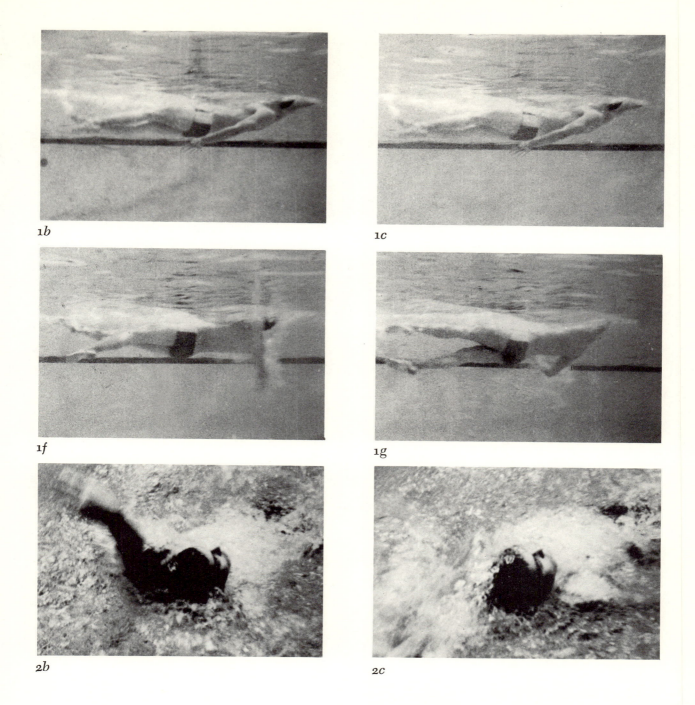

1b

1c

1f

1g

2b

2c

Arm Action

The arm action of the backstroke is perhaps the most graceful and fluid of all strokes. The great backstroker creates the impression of ease and smooth, continuous action. There is a flowing harmony between the two arms. The arms are always in directly opposite phases and moving at the same speed. The stroke never looks rushed.

All propulsion depends on action and reaction. And so it is, of course, with the arm strokes of all swimming, including the backstroke. Our understanding of stroke mechanics is always clearer when we consider the stroke within the framework of action and reaction. What the principle really amounts to is that you go forward by pushing the water backward. The stroke causes the action, and the movement of the body represents the reaction. The desired forward reaction depends both on the amount of action created and its direction. Hence, we try for a pressure against the water that is both powerful and as directly backward as possible.

Somewhat like rowing. The use of the arms in swimming is often compared to the use of oars in rowing a boat. This comparison is especially helpful in understanding the arm action of the backstroke. The similarity of rowing to backstroking is striking, because in both even the direction of your vision is backward. So, the analogy with rowing makes a good starting place for a look at the mechanics of the arm stroke.

At one time the backstroke was actually swum in a way very similar to the way oars are used in rowing a boat. Like oars, the arms were kept straight and they pulled at the same time. The hands described a circular sweeping movement made close to the surface of the water. The back-stroker could really think of himself as rowing a boat. But with progress two important modifications of the original stroke took place. First, alternate arm action replaced the simultaneous pull of both arms. Second, the bent arm stroke replaced the straight arm action.

Alternate stroking. The change from simultaneous arm pulling to alternate action now seems very logical to us. We can easily see the advantage of pulling with one arm while the other arm recovers. Alternate action takes advantage of an important principle of propulsion. Power is most effective when it is evenly applied. When both arms pull at the same time, the total amount of power created can be the same as in alternate arm action, but this power is not efficiently used. Simultaneous pulling makes for a sudden spurt and then a lull, or dead spot. It's like all of the cylinders in an automobile firing at once. In any case, the matter is no longer disputed among fine swimmers. All of them use alternate arm action.

Although alternate arm movement does offer a great and obvious advantage, it also presents a problem. In rowing a boat, alternate pulling on the oars would cause the boat to swerve back and forth, and lateral movement is, of course, inefficient when the job is to go straight ahead. In the same way that alternate rowing strokes produce lateral movement, alternate arm strokes create a tendency for the body to move from side to side. As we will see, this lateral motion is reduced by more efficient arm movement, and whatever lateral-motion potential remains is compensated for by the action of the legs.

Bent-arm pull. The old straight-arm pull gradually gave way to the bent-arm pull. Curiously, a number of good backstrokers still think that they pull with straight arms. Perhaps some do, but slow-motion films demonstrate that nearly all top swimmers use a bent-arm pull.

Let's get back to our comparison of the arm pull and rowing a boat. For the moment we'll consider the blade of the oar, since that is the only part that directly contacts the water. We know that the contribution of blade action to forward propulsion depends upon the blade's speed through the water and its angle relative to the intended direction of boat movement. Our interest is in the angle of the blade rather than its speed. We will assume that the blade is straight up and down in the water, and we can then concentrate on the direction in which the blade is pushing the water.

Remember our principle of action and reaction. The movement of the blade represents the action, and the reaction is in the opposite direction. Thus the blade can be highly efficient in driving the boat forward only when it is pushing the water directly backward. But during the first part of the stroke, the blade is pushing the water partially away from the boat. During the last part of the stroke, though there is a backward component, part of the push of the water is toward the boat.

The oar is designed for reasonably good propulsion, but it does not have high efficiency throughout the stroke. That's because it can't bend to sustain a backward push against the water. But, unlike the oar, the arm can bend. By bending the arm correctly during the stroke, you can gain three advantages. The bent-arm pull allows the pushing action to be more directly backward during a greater part of the stroke. The pushing action takes place closer to the long axis of the body. The bent arm permits a greater mechanical advantage.

Following the arm stroke through a cycle. Correct arm action is smooth and continuous. While one arm is driving through the water, the other is recovering. Looking at one arm, you find it goes through a continuous cycle of drive and recovery. For purposes of analysis a convenient point at which to start following arm action is at the moment of entry. The hand enters the water directly forward of the shoulder. The arm is extended but relaxed. Entry of the hand is knife-like. The palm is held up and down, so the small finger enters the water first and the thumb last.

The recovering arm has an easy, smooth momentum, and upon entry this momentum is maintained. There is no stop. The arm keeps moving. The natural momentum of the arm and a roll of the upper body sink the hand to pulling depth. The catch is made as the hand feels pressure against the water. A loose and flexible shoulder is important for increasing both power and the length of the stroke.

When the hand first enters the water, the arm is momentarily in an awkward position to make a powerful pull. With the arm stretched back, both leverage and muscle structure are unfavorable. But power during the first part of the pull can be increased by the rolling action of the body, which lowers the shoulder, and by the shoulder's flexibility, which allows it to rotate. The shoulder is low and well back so that it can contribute to power.

A good guide to hand position throughout the stroke is the amount of pressure felt on the hand. As soon as the catch is made, pressure should be felt, and the feeling of pressure against the hand should continue until the stroke is completed. Pressure is felt up to the moment of recovery. The more pressure you feel, the more likely it is that you are pushing water directly backward.

As the arm starts to pull, the elbow begins to bend. The bend of the elbow increases until the hand is in line with the shoulder. At this point, with the hand opposite the shoulder, bend is at its greatest. The arm and hand are pushing directly backward. Efficiency of stroke is high. The bending of the elbow raises the hand, but the hand should remain below the surface.

As the hand moves past the shoulder, the arm begins to straighten, and from there on the action becomes a pushing one. The hand easily and smoothly adjusts position so that it continues to push backward. Again, the feeling of pressure on the hand is the guide. You actually do change the action from a pull to a push as the hands move past the shoulders. But there is no stop or break in the movement. The transition is smooth so that there is a continuous flowing action.

The final action of the arm stroke is a whip of the wrist that is both backward and downward. This movement adds propulsive power, but it also has another important purpose. The downward component of the wrist flip helps to rotate the body. The downward push creates an upward reaction. The shoulder on the pushing side becomes higher and thus in a better position to facilitate the recovery. At the same time, the opposite shoulder is driven deeper and in position to make the start of the pull more effective.

Looking at the pattern of the stroke from the side, the underwater path of the hand resembles a horizontal S. Upon entry the hand sinks. It rises during the elbow bend, and the hand is again lowered during the final whip.

The recovery is a necessary preparation for the next stroke, but it should be more than that. The recovery phase gives you a good chance for arm relaxation. By eliminating muscle tension the arm gets an important rest. During recovery the arm is straight, but at the same time it is relaxed. Recovery action is smooth, loose, and rhythmic. No great exertion is needed.

Recovery starts as the final wrist flip ends. The first task is to lift the arm out of the water with the least amount of resistance. Hand position becomes important. The job is to reduce the amount of pressure created by the hand in its upward movement. Any amount of upward pressure has the effect of sinking the body. Hence the hand must be positioned so as to keep its pressure on the water to a minimum. Most fine swimmers turn the hand so that it is straight up and down with the thumb pointing upward. In this position the hand can slice upward and create very little pressure against the water. The action becomes knife-like. Other top back-strokers simply relax the wrist completely. With the wrist limp, the fingers are straight up and down, and, as in the turned hand method, there is little pressure against the water.

When the arm leaves the water, it moves straight upward. The path of the recovery is vertical and directly in line with the body. The vertical path during recovery works out best, despite the arguments presented against it. Some swimmers feel that a lateral path in which the arm recovers close to the body saves energy. There is some theoretical justification for the view that some energy can be saved by keeping the arm low during recovery. However, the disadvantage is that lateral action tends to produce lateral reaction. A sideways recovery creates a force that drives the body out of alignment so that drag is increased. In short, the small gain in energy saving accomplished by skimming the arm along the water is more than lost by the increased resistance to the water. So, all in all, it's better to recover the arm in a straight up-and-down path.

The action of the arms is smooth, flowing, and continuous. With the completion of the recovery another cycle begins. The recovery brings the arm forward of the shoulder. And during the recovery the hand turns easily and smoothly so that the little finger enters the water first. There is no stop. Momentum is continued. The hand slices through the water, sinking to pulling depth. The catch is made, and the arm pull is under way.

An analysis of stroke mechanics is important to you, as it is to all ambitious athletes. An understanding of the physics involved does provide the basis for acquiring correct action. But all effective athletic movements must appear smooth and natural. So it is with the arm action of the backstroke. The points of technique are blended together to produce an action of rhythm and smoothness.

3. The introduction of alternate arm action was a big advance in backstroke technique. Because one arm is always pulling, application of power is steady and therefore more effective.

3a

3e

3d

4a

4. The arms bend during the pull. Maximum bend is reached when the hands pass by the shoulders. From there on the arms begin to straighten.

4d

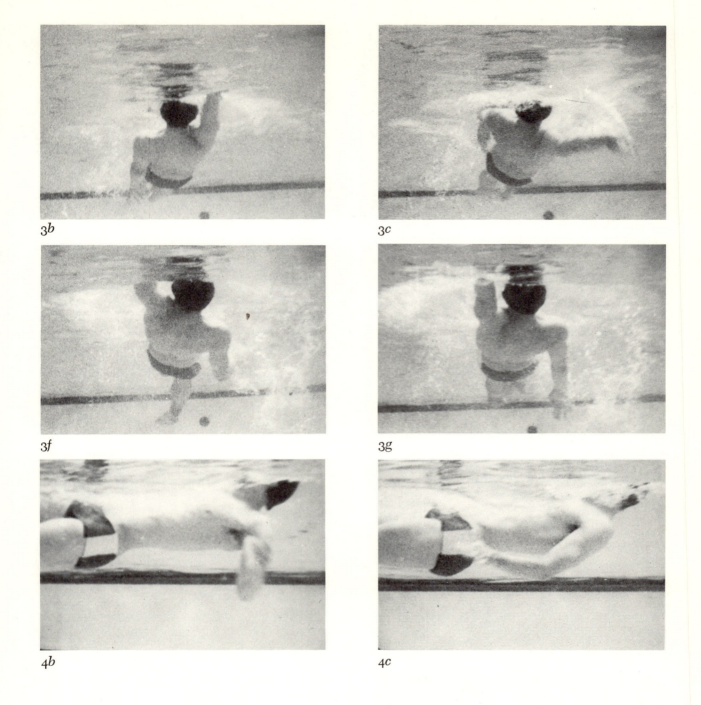

3b

3c

3f

3g

4b

4c

5. The entry and hand catch.

5*a*

6. A cycle of the arm action. The right arm is halfway through the pull while the left arm recovers (*a*, *b*, and *c*). The left hand catches (*d*). A roll of the body lowers the shoulder (*e* and *f*) and puts the arm in a better pulling position. The left arm continues its pull while the right arm recovers. As the left arm finishes its driving action, the right hand makes its entry (*h*). The cycle continues with the right arm pulling and the left arm recovering.

6*a*

6*d*

6*e*

6*h*

6*i*

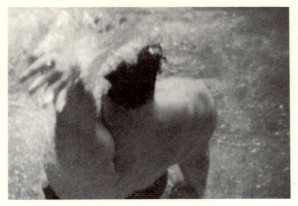

5*b*

6*b*

6*c*

6*f*

6*g*

6*j*

6*k*

7. Power is added to the arm pull by the roll and flexibility of the shoulder. The shoulder is deep and well back.

7a

8. The last part of the arm action as shown in a dry-land demonstration. Action is both backward and downward.

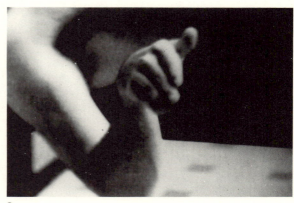

8a

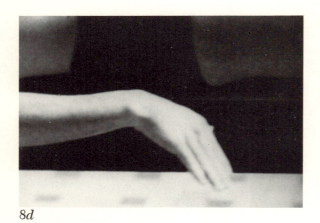

8d

9. During the recovery the arm is straight and moves in a vertical path. Relaxation is important. Note the limp wrist (b).

9a

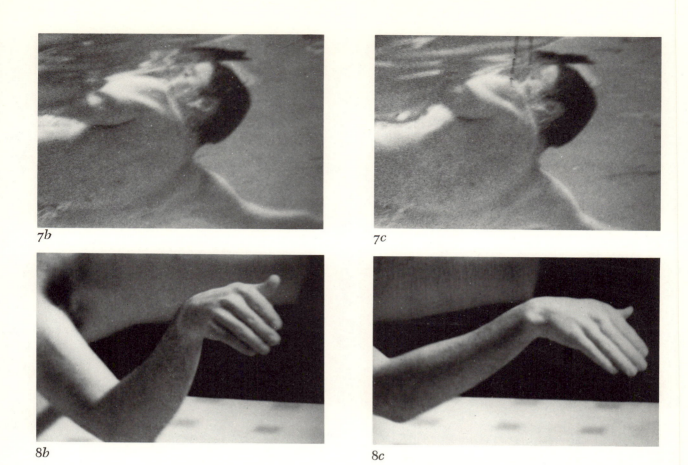

7b

7c

8b

8c

9b

9c

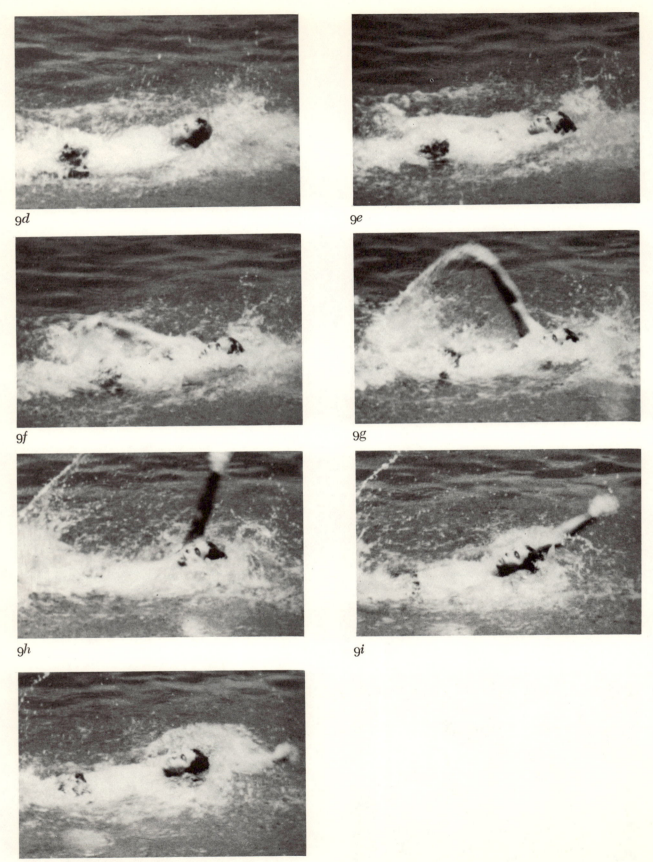

9d

9e

9f

9g

9h

9i

9j

Kicking

Like the arms, the legs supply propulsion by pushing the water backward. By driving backward against the water, the legs create a reaction that helps to move the body forward. The principle used to guide effective action in the kick is the same as for the arm pull. We are still dealing with the basic principle that action and reaction are in opposite directions. Hence, we want the action of the legs to be as much backward as possible. Also, since action and reaction have the same strength, we want the action to be as powerful as possible.

Coaches often compare the leg action of the backstroke with that of the sprint crawl carried out upside down. There are indeed similarities between the two kicks. The timing is the same in that almost all good backstrokers swim a six-beat stroke—that is, there are six kicks for every two arm strokes. The basic difference between the kicks of the two strokes lies in their sources of real power. In the crawl the greater power is generated during the downbeat, and in the backstroke the greater power comes during the upbeat of the legs. The truly significant feature of similarity of the two strokes is that the kicks require flexibility of the joints. The ankles and feet must remain loose. It is looseness that makes for the flipper-like action so necessary to forward propulsion.

The foot is the "blade." In all sports that depend on speed of propulsion, what ultimately matters is the speed of the extremities. In kicking we are talking about the speed of the feet. All action should build up to the speed of the feet. The big muscles of the body, including those of the legs, supply the real power, but this large muscle power is effective only when it expresses itself in foot speed.

The general idea of using the big muscles of the body to create speed in the extremities can be seen in other sports activities. For example, the baseball pitcher makes full use of his body, but the speed of the ball is determined by how fast his hand is moving at the instant the ball is released. A closer example is found in track and field. Sprinters are powerful people whose technique training is concerned mostly with making the best use of their power. This power has to express itself in fast movement of the feet. The feet themselves don't have power. It's simply that power developed by the large muscles has to result in the fast movement of the feet.

To summarize this important principle, when we are dealing with speed of propulsion, whether it concerns the body itself or any other object, it is the speed of the relevant extremities that matters. It is vital that all needed trunk and limb muscles play a part, but their function is to create speed in the extremities.

The value of the kick. The contribution of the kick to the backstroke (and crawl, too) has been questioned by a number of leading authorities. Some experts claim that the kick has no value. Others say that the kick can actually reduce swimming speed. The controversy still exists, but it can be resolved simply. An effective kick does contribute to propulsion. An ineffective kick does not. What is the test of an effective kick? The main criteria have to be the speed of the feet and the direction in which they are pushing the water.

How fast should the feet be moving? Obviously, the faster the better. But we can pinpoint exactly how fast the feet have to go in order to contribute to forward propulsion. Let's return to our picture of the foot as the blade of the oar. Imagine that you are pulling an oar in a boat that is moving at ten miles per hour. Now when are you making a contribution to the boat's speed and when are you hindering the boat's speed? It all depends on the speed at which you get the blade moving through the water. If you simply stick the oar in the water, you know that you are going to cause a drag. If you pull slowly, you will reduce the amount of drag, but it will still be there. If you get the blade of your oar moving backward at ten miles per hour, you no longer cause drag. But you don't help either. When your blade exceeds a speed of ten miles an hour, you start to make a contribution to the propulsion of the boat. A principle can be stated. In order for the blade to contribute, its backward speed has to be greater than the forward speed of the vessel.

To carry our analogy further, the body can be looked upon as the boat. The arms are the main source of propulsion and by themselves can give a certain speed to the body. The extent to which the kick can contribute to forward propulsion depends on the speed at which the feet move and the direction in which they push the water. In order to help, the feet must move backward at a speed greater than the forward speed of the body. You can see that a good use of the legs can increase swimming speed and that a poor kick can actually decrease speed. Hence, the importance of correct technique in carrying out the kick.

Pattern of the kick. As in the crawl stroke, the kick of the backstroke is mainly up and down. The range through which this vertical action takes place is from approximately two feet below the surface to a level just below the surface. Neither the knees nor the feet actually break the surface.

As mentioned, the backstroke kick is upside down in comparison to the crawl kick. In the crawl kick the downbeat supplies the greater power. As you might expect, it's the upbeat that gives the greater power in the backstroke kick. That's because of the structure of the leg. During the upbeat the leg starts in a bent position and then straightens. The straightening of the leg is brought about by the powerful extensor muscles of the thigh. In this way great velocity of the foot can be developed.

The kicking action is continuous. While one leg kicks upward, the other leg kicks downward. It doesn't make too much difference where we start in describing the action. However, as a convenient starting point we can begin with the completion of the upbeat. At this point, the leg is completely straightened. Because the instep has been the blade, the toes still point backward. Now the leg starts downward. Two features are highly important. First, the leg remains straight. It is even more effective if the leg hyper-extends—that is, if the leg tends to bend the other way. Such an upward bend obviously can only be slight, but some swimmers do get an advantage from their unusual flexibility. Second, the foot changes its angle. As the leg starts downward, there is a bend at the ankle so that the sole of the foot is almost directly toward the rear. As always, flexibility becomes of great importance. A loose ankle allows the foot to adjust so that the sole becomes a more effective blade.

As the downbeat is completed, the knee starts to bend. The thigh drives upward, and because of the bend at the knee the foot drops slightly. In other words, in the initial stage of the upward kick, the upper leg and the foot are actually moving in opposite directions. The upper leg is going up, and the foot is going down. But these movements come about naturally, and they prepare the foot for a buildup of velocity.

The upbeat should be a very powerful kick. Carried out correctly, the action is similar to that of the full instep kick used in soccer. There is a movement of the leg from the hip to supply basic power. Then there is a straightening of the leg, which supplies snap. At this point, there should be great speed of the foot. To carry further the comparison with the strongest of soccer kicks, the instep or front of the foot is the point of impact. The instep should be moving as fast as possible and driving the water backward.

Foot position is highly critical to producing an effective kick. During the downbeat the sole of the foot is the pushing surface. During the upbeat it's the instep or top of the foot that acts as the blade. You can see that flexion must shift at the beginnings of both the downward and upward actions. Correct movement of the foot does not depend so much on a conscious effort to bend the foot upward or downward. Rather, the effective positioning of the foot is brought about by looseness of the ankle. Looseness is all-important. If the ankle is loose enough, this looseness tends to position the foot automatically in the correct angle.

For purposes of analysis we've regarded the kick as taking place in the vertical plane. This isn't completely so except in kicking drills. The arm action requires a certain amount of rotation of the body, and the legs respond to this rotation by kicking at slight angles to the vertical. Yet the basic principles of kicking remain the same.

10. The backstroke kick can be regarded as an upside-down version of the crawl kick. Both strokes have a six-beat kick. But the main power of the backstroke kick comes from the upbeat.

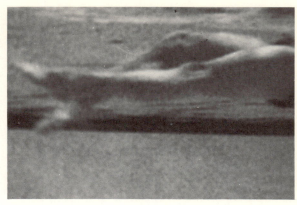

10*a*

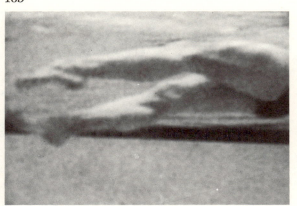

10*b*

10*c*

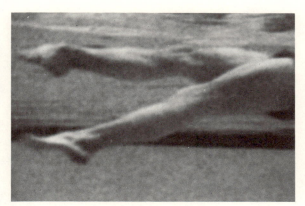

10*d*

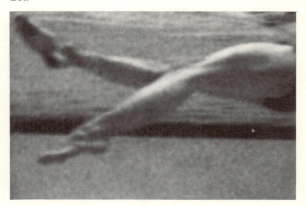

10*e*

10*f*

11. The right leg followed through a kicking cycle. The knee lifts while the foot is still moving downward. The leg starts to straighten (*b*). The powerful extensor muscles of the leg build up to a terrific snap of the foot (*c*). Note the turbulence created by the speed of the foot. The leg is straight or even hyper-extended as it starts downward. The cycle starts again (*f* and *g*).

11*a*

11*d*

11*e*

12*a*

12. The kicking action has to adjust to the roll of the body. Hence, the action is not entirely in the vertical plane.

12*d*

12*e*

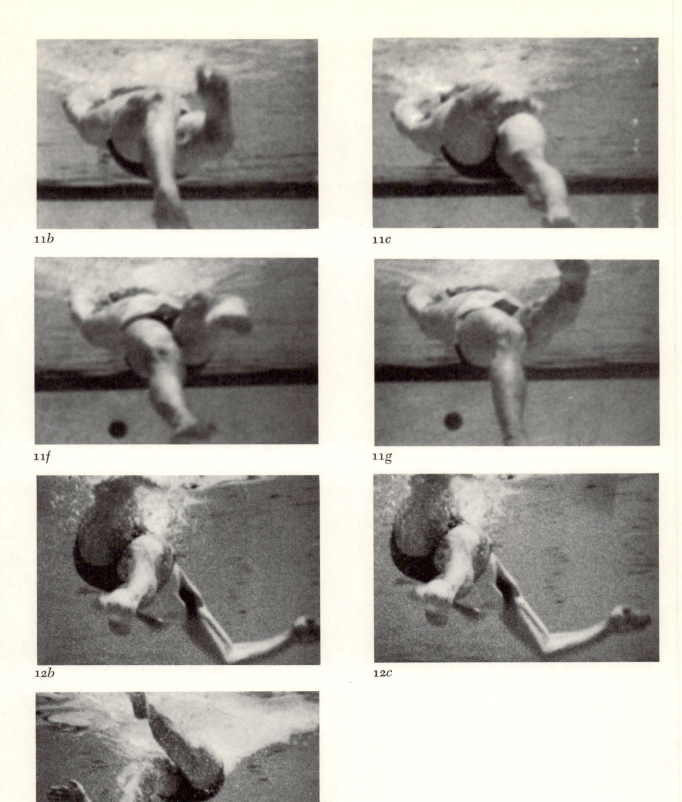

11*b*

11*c*

11*f*

11*g*

12*b*

12*c*

12*f*

The Start

Two striking features of the backstroke start make it different from the other racing starts. Unlike the starting positions of the other three strokes, the starting position in the backstroke faces you away from the direction in which you are going to swim. And instead of starting above the deck of the pool, you start with part of your body in the water. Even though the backstroke start requires different techniques, the goals are the same as for other strokes:

(1) A quick reaction at the sound of the gun. As soon as the gun sounds you want to get going. Your ability to move quickly will depend partly on your natural reaction time, but concentration and good technique are needed.

(2) Power off the wall. You want a solid leg drive that will generate initial speed.

(3) A streamlined position upon entry. You want to enter the water so as to preserve the speed developed by your drive from the wall.

(4) Favorable position in the water. After entering the water, you want to achieve a body position that both sustains initial momentum and gets you ready to start swimming.

On your mark. Just before the command of "Take your mark," the starting bar is grasped, and the feet are positioned against the wall. In most meets, and especially the bigger ones, you can count on a bar or grips for your hands. However, in some of your early and smaller meets standard gripping facilities may not be there. You may have to improvise. So, even if your own practice pool has a bar or grips, it is a good idea to get in some starting without them—just in case.

The rules governing placement of the feet vary. The basic difference is that the American college and high school rules require only that part of the feet be underwater, whereas AAU and international rules require that the feet be entirely underwater at the start.

The feet are placed solidly and comfortably against the wall. The placement must be very solid. You can't afford to slip during the leg drive. Spacing between feet is about six inches. Comfort is the main consideration. Most fine backstrokers find it best to have both feet at the same level. Yet some world-class swimmers like to have one foot somewhat lower than the other. This was true of a number of finalists at the 1972 Olympic Games.

At the command "Take your mark," you draw yourself upward so that your trunk is erect, with your head about a foot from the starting platform. The hips are still partially in the water. As you pull your body upward, make sure that your feet maintain their solid contact with the wall. In pulling yourself into the "set" position, the movements are slow and smooth. There is no delay calculated to obtain an unfair advantage, but quick and jerky movements are eliminated. You should be coiled and ready to strike, but not tense. The optimum amount of leg bend depends on leg strength. The stronger your legs the deeper their bend. Now is the time for full concentration, for readiness to move at the sound of the gun.

At the gun. An effective start is a coordinated act that involves the entire body—legs, arms, trunk, and head. When the gun sounds, the arms and legs drive. The body changes position, and the head draws backward. The coordination among these actions is important but not too difficult if the over-all goals of the start are kept in mind.

A good part of the arm action is actually completed before the feet leave the wall. At the gun, the arms drive against the grips and continue to swing. The path of the arms is relatively low with the hands remaining below shoulder height. The arms continue their swing until they are back of the head.

The arm swing has a number of important functions. First, a vigorous push and a strong swing create power that helps both in moving the body farther outward and in producing greater speed upon entry. Second, the swing helps to control body position and direction. Third, the swing ends with the arms placed in a good position for a streamlined entry. At the time of entering the water, the head is between the arms. The arms are straight with the hands close together.

Body position changes from the gun to entry. While awaiting the gun the body is flexed with the head in a normal position. At the gun the head moves backward, and the body begins to straighten. The body continues to straighten and then goes beyond the straight position so that it is actually somewhat arched upon entry.

The legs are, of course, the great source of starting power. The pushing muscles of the legs are very strong, and, as they straighten, an enormous thrust can be developed. Since the drive is against the wall, a firm and solid contact by the feet becomes all-important. Any slipping of the feet would be costly. That's why the placing and feel of the feet against the wall deserve a great deal of practice attention.

The timing between leg drive and arm swing tends to come about rather naturally. The arms move faster than the legs, because once the hands leave the grips, the arms meet very little resistance. In contrast, the legs carry out a sustained drive against the wall. As a result, the arms have almost finished their action before the feet break contact with the wall. From the standpoint of physics this is a good arrangement, because it increases the power contribution of the arms.

Height. In contrast to other swimmers who start above the deck, the backstroker must create his own height. A certain amount of height is needed, but the beginner tends to become obsessed with height. The great backstrokers are more concerned with distance, power, and position. Experience has shown that the right amount of height brings the hips just clear of the surface. The feet remain in the water. Body height is controlled primarily by the initial action of the arms. There are two components to the arm drive against the grips. The push is both downward and away from the body. The amount of downward drive determines body height. So you can increase or decrease body height by changing the amount of downward pressure exerted by the arms.

Your coach can readily observe excessive height. You can recognize it, too, because it will give you the feeling of dropping on the water and losing momentum. The correct amount of height will let you spear into the water without interruption of movement. The common error is on the side of too much height.

The backstroke start does not lend itself as easily to a knife-like entry as do the other starts. Still, the backstroke entry should be as streamlined as possible. The back is arched. The head is back and between the outstretched arms. The hands are together and make the first contact with the water.

After entry. Once you have entered the water, there must be a rapid adjustment in body position. Unlike other swimmers, the backstroker enters the water with his back arched and his head thrown back. This entry position is needed. But if this arched position were held after entry, the swimmer would be driven too deeply into the water. Body position has to change away from the arched position. Actually, the shift in position is not very difficult. It just takes poise. Once underwater, if the chin is dropped toward the chest, the needed changes in body position take place smoothly and almost automatically.

As in all starts, swimming begins when the speed generated by the push off the wall slows down until it equals swimming speed. Since the backstroke start is less powerful than the other starts, swimming starts sooner. Yet it is still important to remain calm and poised. There is never a wild scramble to begin the stroke. The kick and arm pull can start together. But in actual practice most backstrokers find it more effective to kick first and then pull.

13. Although different in technique, the backstroke start has the same goals as other starts—a quick reaction to the gun, a powerful leg drive, and a streamlined position of the body.

13*a*

13*b*

13*c*

14. Getting ready for the start. The bar is grasped without tension. Movement into position is smooth and relaxed. The arms have two jobs to do. They hold the body in position and then help with the drive at the sound of the gun.

14a

14d

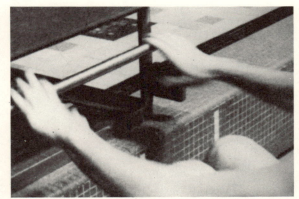

14e

15. Solid and comfortable placement of the feet against the wall before the start. Because the legs are the main source of starting power, the contact of the feet must be firm.

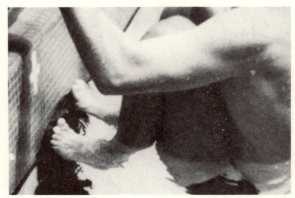

15a

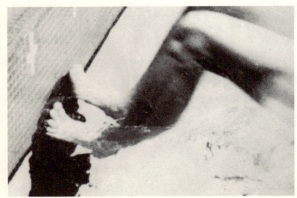

15d

15e

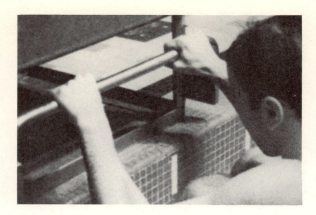

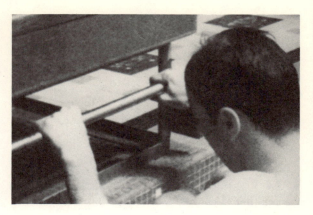

14b

14c

14f

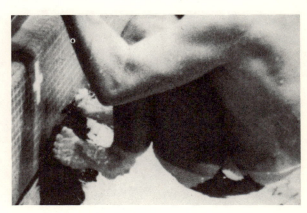

15b

15c

16a

16. The body remains well in the water even as the "take your mark" position is assumed.

17a

17. The arms smoothly and easily pull the body into the "take your mark" position. The body is alert but relaxed. Unlike other starts, the backstroke start takes place in the water. Needed height during the drive after the sound of the gun has to be created by the drive off the marks. Excessive height should be avoided. Correct height lifts the hips just clear of the water while the lower legs remain in the water.

17d

17e

18a

18. The arms play a key role in the start. Their drive is sideways and parallel to the water.

16b

16c

17b

17c

17f

17g

18b

18c

19. The legs are the great source of power in starting.

19*a*

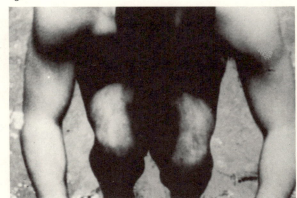

19*b*

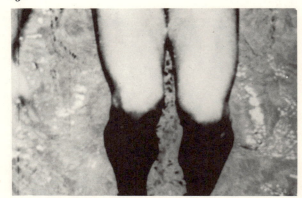

19*c*

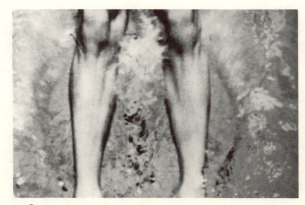

19*d*

The Turn

The turn in the backstroke requires a somewhat different technique from that used with the other strokes. That's because the rules limit what can be done. Yet, although specific techniques must be used to stay within the rules, the basic goals of the backstroke turn are the same as for all turns: speed and power.

The turn should always be viewed as an opportunity to increase speed, as a chance to gain an advantage. At the end of each pool length you have a solid wall to work with. This solid surface makes possible a mighty push that should drive you through the water at a speed greater than that of normal swimming. A well-executed turn is really more than an opportunity—it's a must. Hence, the need for a clear understanding of what you are doing and for faithful practice to carry out an effective turn under the pressure of competition.

Rules. The rules set up the conditions under which the turn can be made, and in this way they affect the technique that can be used. The rules are not complicated at all. They are, in fact, reasonable enough. Their one and simple purpose is to make sure that the race remains a backstroke contest.

The rules require that you stay on your back until you touch the wall. And you must return to your back before leaving the wall. The definition of being on "the back" is as follows. You must not "turn over beyond the vertical toward the breast." That's quite a bit of leeway. You can actually turn halfway around before touching the wall. Once having touched the wall, you are free to use any method of turning that you wish. After the touch, your body can be in any position. But before leaving the wall you have to return to "the back" position.

Approach to the wall. In competition you must be able to approach the wall at full racing speed. Though timing is important, it should not be at the expense of speed. You practice to become both accurate and fast in reaching the wall. The backstroke is the one stroke in which normal swimming position affords no forward view. With the head in correct position its' impossible to see the wall.

The overhead flags supply orientation. These flags are above you and five yards from the wall. Looking up at the flags lets you know where you are and gets you ready to make the touch. The polished backstroker who gets well oriented toward the flags doesn't have to look for the wall at all. But the average swimmer usually sneaks in a quick look just prior to the touch. As the wall is neared, the arm that is making the recovery is the natural one for the touch. But you can't be sure which arm will be recovering when the touch is to be made. If you become used to touching always with the same arm, there will be many times when you will have to slow swimming speed to make the touch. For this reason the great backstrokers practice to become equally comfortable in touching with either hand.

The spin turn: We will be considering two extreme ways of turning. First, let's look at the spin turn. In this method the turning takes place almost entirely in the horizontal plane. It's almost as if you were lying across a swivel chair on your back. As the chair rotates, you make a complete turnabout. And during the turn your body remains nearly flat or in the horizontal plane. Because you remain on your back during the spin, there is practically no likelihood of violating the rules. You approach the wall on your back, turn on your back, and leave the wall on your back.

The early action of the touching arm is the same as it would be for normal recovery. That is, the arm takes its normal swing of upward and backward. Ideal timing would be as follows. Just as the arm completes its normal recovery action, it would make contact with the wall. The other arm would be just completing its stroke. As the touching arm reaches the wall, it bends or gives. The touching arm is used both for timing the body's distance from the wall and to help in the turning.

The arm contact with the wall starts the turn. The body flexes so that the legs rise. At the same time, the turn continues. In this way the action of the legs is both upward and sideways. The legs turn and lift so that the lower part of the legs rises above the surface. The non-touching arm helps to propel the body through its spin.

The flexion of the body is important in speeding up the spin. The long axis of the body becomes shortened. In this way you become more compact and turn more quickly and easily. It's easier to turn a rowboat than it is to turn an ocean liner.

As the turn nears completion, the legs begin to lower. They drop until the feet are below the surface and in firm contact with the wall. At the time that they make contact with the wall, the legs are flexed in readiness for a powerful drive. Meanwhile, the arms have completed their job of helping with the turn, the touching arm by pushing off the wall, and the other arm by a paddling action. Now the arms are ready to move to a streamlined position. They are straightened and placed in the direction of swimming, hands close together, head between the hands. This streamlining is further completed by a straightening of the upper body. The trunk is both straight and parallel to the surface of the water. The body is positioned to take full advantage of the leg drive off the wall. A hard drive straightens the legs. The body maintains its streamlined position. As in all turns, the speed on leaving the wall should be faster than swimming speed. That means that swimming starts only when the glide speed slows down to swimming speed.

Tumble or somersault turn. The terms "tumble turn" and "somersault turn" mean about the same thing. The turn we are talking about now is faster than the spin turn. But it's much riskier, and disqualification is frequent. As we describe the tumble turn, you will see why it is both fast and risky.

When there are for practical purposes no restrictions to the method of turning, the somersault (or, more accurately, the half somersault) turn is the fastest way of getting around. This kind of turn is used by all top freestylers. There are two main reasons for the great speed of this turn. First, the body can almost be rolled into a ball. The turning radius of the body is short during the consequent quick rotation. Second, the turning action takes place along the direction of swimming, making for less loss of energy.

As indicated, the somersault in the turn is really half of a somersault. You can see that by examining the photos of turns. Also, you can quickly figure out that a full somersault would not do any good. Instead of producing a turn, it would keep you going in the same direction as before. A half somersault reverses your direction, but a pure half somersault also turns you upside down. If you start a half somersault on your stomach, you'll end up on your back. Conversely, if you start on your back, you will end up on your stomach.

The only way to solve the problem of ending up in the right body position is to rotate the body during the turn. The somersault turn would be at its greatest efficiency if you could rotate to your stomach before the touch. But you can't. The rules require that you "must not turn over beyond the vertical toward the breast before the foremost hand has touched the end of the pool." You know that rotation is going to be needed. So the goal is to rotate as far as possible toward the vertical without breaking the rules. The body rotation starts before the touch is made. At the point where the touch is actually made, the body cannot have rotated beyond the vertical. Timing is critical. If rotation is less than allowed by the rules, there is a loss of efficiency. And, of course, if rotation is more than allowed there is disqualification. This is the only point in the turn where disqualification is truly a problem. There is no problem coming off the wall.

After the touch is made, rotation continues along with the somersault. From here on until the wall is left there are no rules restrictions. During the somersault the body is tucked or flexed. The somersault brings the legs above the water's surface. The legs continue to move and descend until the feet are in firm contact with the wall. Timing should be such that the body is the right distance from the wall. That means that your legs are flexed and ready for a powerful push. Because of your body's rotation—part of it before the somersault and the remainder during the somersault—you are already on your back when it is time to drive off the wall. You can benefit from your practice in making other turns, because there are common factors. As in all turns, it's important that the legs be flexed and solidly positioned against the wall. The more powerful the leg drive against the wall the greater the speed. Streamlined body position makes the best use of the momentum generated by the leg drive off the wall. When glide speed drops to swimming speed, then swimming starts.

In the tumble or somersault turn the turning forces are somewhat different from those in the spin turn. The spin turn depends heavily on use of the arms. Turning depends mostly on the touching arm pushing against the wall, while the other arm paddles. In contrast, the turning forces for the somersault turn are set up by shifting body position. By diving and raising your legs, you create water resistance that tends to spin you around in the vertical plane.

Which turn? Two types of turns are available. One is safe. The other is faster but riskier. It may take some experimentation. You and your coach will talk it over. Since the spin turn is made entirely on your back, this way of turning presents no risk of disqualification. The tumble or somersault turn has only one risky spot—just as the touch is being made. You are not allowed to go beyond the vertical until the touch is actually made. After that point, there is no further risk of disqualification, because the half somersault puts you on your back before you leave the wall.

Most champions are masters of both turns. If they think that the officiating will be sharp and discerning, they tend to use the tumble turn. If they think otherwise, they are prepared to use the safer spin turn. No matter which turn is selected, it has to be practiced and polished. That means lots of work and close cooperation with your coach.

20. The overhead flags, hung five yards from the wall, guide the timing of the turn.

21. An over-all view of the spin turn. The touch (*b*, *c*, and *d*), and turning action of the touching arm. The legs touch solidly against the wall (*e*). The powerful leg drive (*f* and *g*) builds up speed that is conserved by a streamlined position of the body.

21*a*

21*d*

21*e*

21*h*

21*i*

21*b*

21*c*

21*f*

21*g*

22. The spin turn demonstrated on dry land. The touch is made (*a*). The touching arm starts to bend, and the legs begin to draw up (*b*). The body starts to spin (*e*). With the completion of the spin, the legs position themselves for the drive (*f—k*).

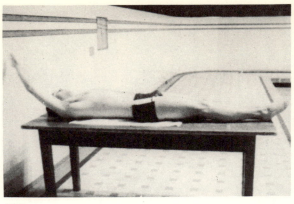

22*a*

22*d*

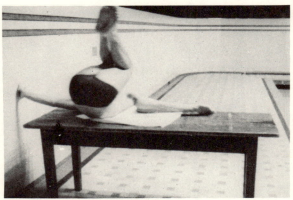

22*e*

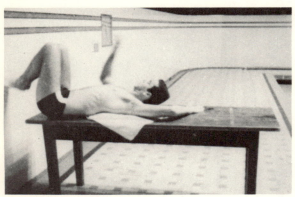

22*h*

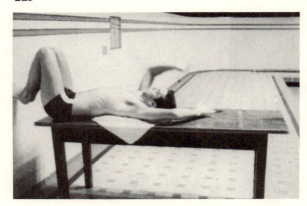

22*i*

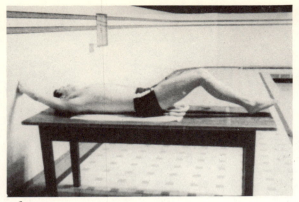

22b

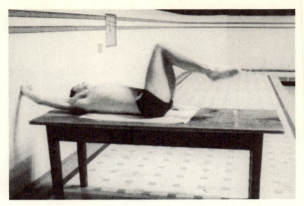

22c

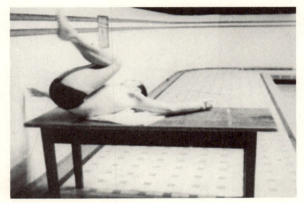

22f

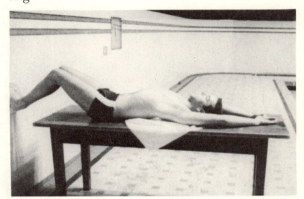

22g

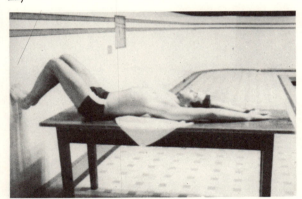

22j

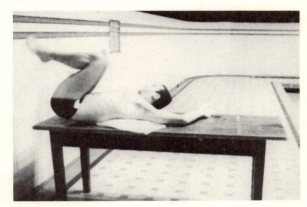

22k

23. The spin turn is safe because it is carried out on the back. The touching arm is used to help spin the body (*b*). The turning radius is shortened by flexing at the hips (*c, d,* and *e*). The lower legs rise above the surface and then descend to drive against the wall (*f* and *g*). The body is streamlined to make the most of the speed generated off the wall (*h*). The start of swimming (*i*).

23*a*

23*d*

23*e*

23*h*

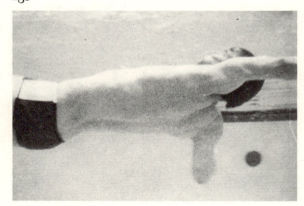

23*i*

23b

23c

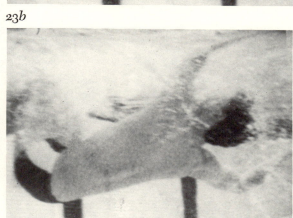

23f

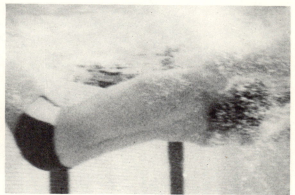

23g

24. A well-executed turn produces power off the wall. Initial speed is greater than swimming speed. Patience and poise are needed to hold a streamlined position. This position is held until the glide speed slows to swimming speed.

24a

24d

24e

24h

24i

24b

24c

24f

24g

24j

25. The sequence of the fast but risky somersault turn. As the wall is approached, rotation of the body has already started (*a*). At the point of touch (*b*), rotation has brought the body near the vertical, but not beyond it. After the turn is made (*c*), rotation continues and the half-somersault begins. Rotation is completed (*e*). During the tumble the feet rise above the surface and then reach the wall (*j*). The legs drive powerfully (*k* and *l*), and the glide begins.

25*a*

25*d*

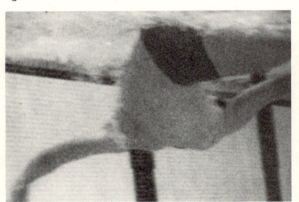

25*e*

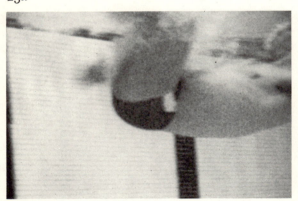

25*h*

25*i*

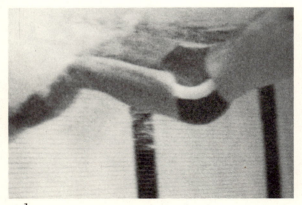

25*l*

25*m*

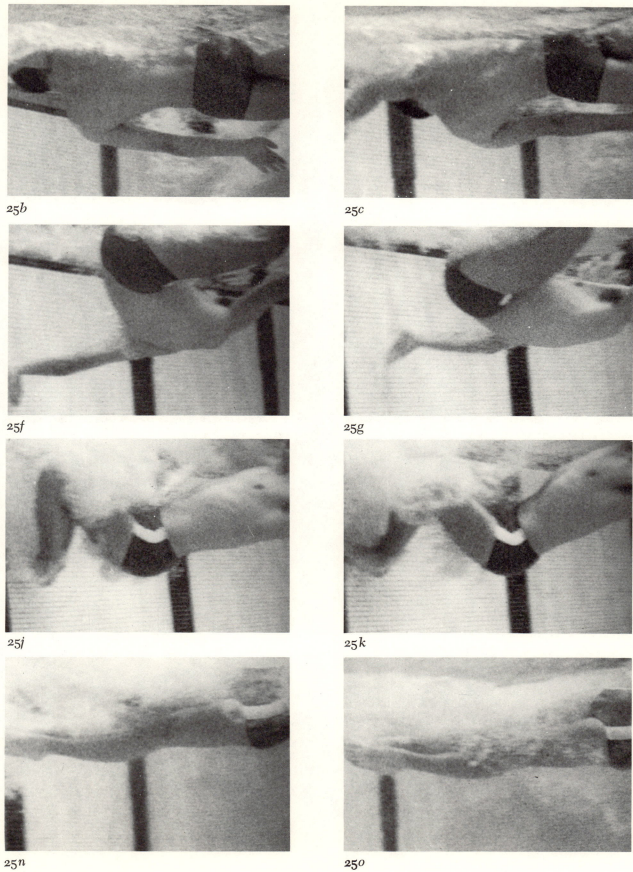

25*b*

25*c*

25*f*

25*g*

25*j*

25*k*

25*n*

25*o*

26a

26. The great speed of the somersault turn results from the compact position of the body and the fact that turning takes place along the vertical plane. The arms position themselves to increase streamlining (*f* and *g*).

26d

26e

27. The point of risk in the tumble turn is just before the touch. There is the danger of rotating past the vertical. Once the touch has been safely made, there should be no further risk of disqualification. The half-somersault puts the body squarely on the back.

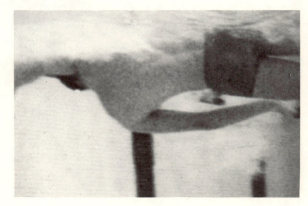

27a

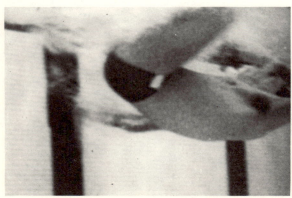

27d

27e

26b

26c

26f

26g

27b

27c

27f

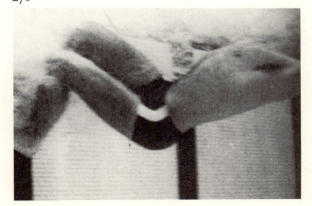

27g

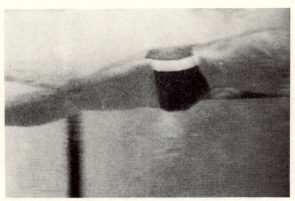

27h

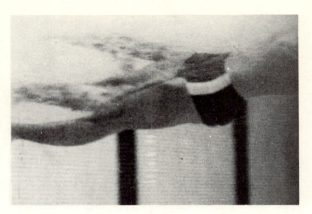

27i

IV. Breaststroke Swimming

Introduction

The breaststroke is an "early" stroke in every way. Of the four competitive strokes, the breaststroke is by far the oldest, and it is almost always the first stroke for the new swimmer. It has had a long and interesting history. For at least hundreds of years swimmers have propelled themselves with a stroke that is somewhat similar to our present breaststroke. Of course, modern experts have developed refinements to make the stroke faster, but its modern descendant clearly resembles the breaststroke of the old days.

The breaststroke was well suited for lakes, rivers, and oceans where the swimmer could expect to cope with rough water. The stroke could also be used with comfort and with less effort than other methods. Also, the breaststroke allowed the swimmer to keep his head out of the water. In this way he could breathe more readily and, at the same time, see where he was going.

As competitive swimming became more popular, the old advantages offered by the breaststroke became unimportant to the competitor. The name of the game became speed. Since the swimmer could swim any way he wanted to, newer and faster strokes came into use. This trend culminated in the development of the crawl stroke and the temporary disappearance of the breaststroke from serious competition. But the breaststroke was destined to return again as a racing stroke. During the early part of this century, separate classes were set up for the three strokes then in competitive use. With this arrangement the breaststroke race became a distinct event with its own rules.

The breaststroke was to face two more threats to its place in competitive swimming. The first of the threats was underwater swimming. Experimenting coaches and athletes found that they could move faster under water than on the surface. Japanese swimmers became especially adept at the underwater stroke and would often swim a complete lap under water. For a time the underwater swimmers, and particularly the Japanese, dominated the breaststroke. This domination was lost when in 1957 the rules outlawed underwater swimming except for one stroke at the start and one stroke after each turn.

The second threat to the breaststroke came out of Brooklyn, New York, in 1933. A breaststroker began experimenting with an over-water recovery of the arms. By bringing his arms out of the water during recovery, his movement was faster because he met less water resistance. The new method really worked. The increase in speed was spectacular. The first use of the new recovery caused a storm of protests from swimmers, coaches, 'and officials. But the new method apparently was perfectly legal. It could not be beaten, so it was joined. Other swimmers began to use it. Because of its appearance this new variation was called the "butterfly." This stroke proved to be so effective that in time the orthodox breaststroker had no chance against a proficient "flyer." Eventually the rules were changed so that the butterfly stroke was split off as a separate event. Once more the ancient breaststroke was saved.

You can see that the breaststroke has had a difficult time keeping alive as a competitive stroke. Because swimmers are naturally always on the alert for an "edge," there is only one way that this fine old stroke can be preserved in competitive racing: the rules have to be strict. The rules are indeed strict, and they are enforced. Disqualification is frequent. An important part of the breaststrokers' practice sessions is centered on making sure that his technique is within the rules. Actually, the rules are not all that complicated, and if you follow good training procedures, you won't find the rules to be a hardship.

Body Position

No matter what the swimming stroke, body position is critical. It won't do to have even enormous power negated by poor body position. The speed of anything moving through the water, whether fish, boat, or human being, is determined by two basic factors: propulsion and resistance. Propulsion depends on the amount of power applied and how efficiently it is applied. The resistance of the water, assuming a certain amount of propulsive power, determines the final speed. The more streamlined the body, the less the drag—and the greater the speed.

In designing a ship, naval architects are highly concerned with the problem of water resistance. They know that if the ship has undue drag, speed is cut, power is wasted. So they reduce water resistance through careful and scientific attention to streamlining. Nearly every fish that can be observed today is a marvel of streamlining, as a result of natural selection. Those primeval fish that may not have been streamlined did not survive. They were not fast enough either to eat or to keep from being eaten. The human swimmer cannot redesign his body, nor can he evolve as the fish did. He just has to use his body in such a way that water resistance is cut to a minimum.

Good body position can be described rather simply. But there is an enormous contrast between the few words that describe body position and the great importance of body position to the swimmer. The basics are: (1) the body should remain as close as possible to the horizontal, and (2) the body should stay in alignment with the direction in which it is going.

There are only two simple ideas. In other words, the body should stay as flat as you can keep it while still carrying on the business of swimming. And the body should not swerve from side to side. It should stay pointed straight ahead. Although the description of correct body position is simple, acquiring effective body position is not all that easy. It takes constant practice and checking by your coach or other observer.

One of the complexities in achieving correct body position is that you have to use parts of the body for propulsion. In the case of a ship the propellers turn without affecting the streamlining of the hull. The shape of the ship obviously remains the same. But in human swimming the needed propulsive movements require some compromise of the most effective body position. Driving with the arms and legs has to cause a certain amount of interference with the streamlining of the body. The goal is to make the best and most efficient use of the arms and legs for forward power and still keep body resistance to the water as low as possible.

In summary, body position should get direct and conscious attention. We want to keep the body fairly flat and in alignment with forward direction. Although we pay direct attention to body position, we also have to keep checking the stroke for its effects on body position.

The height at which the head is held strongly affects streamlining. Streamlining is best when the face is in the water. But of course the head has to be lifted when a breath is taken. The solution is to lift your head only as high as needed to breathe in, and then get your face back in the water as quickly as you can. Breathing is timed with arm action, so we will be talking more about breathing when we get to the section on the arm pull.

The Arms

In arm action, as in other parts of the breaststroke, the first consideration is to stay within the rules. As you know, the spirit and the intent of the rules are clear: to preserve the breaststroke as a competitive event. During recovery both hands must be pushed forward together from the breast. As the hands move forward, they can be either on or under the water—but not above the water. In all their movements the arms must move simultaneously and their action must be symmetrical; that is, the pattern of one arm is almost the mirror image of the other.

Basic goal. The goal of arm action in the breaststroke is the same as that of other strokes. You try to push the water as directly backward as you can. Movement comes about by action and reaction. You push or pull against the water (action), and the body moves (reaction). The important principle is that reaction is always directly opposite in direction from that of the action. If you push downward on the water, your body tends to lift. If you push upward, you lower your body. So you see that the most efficient push is a backward one, since it drives you forward. The technique of arm action makes much more sense when we keep in mind the basic goal—to push the water as directly backward as possible.

The main pushing surfaces are the hands and the forearms. These areas make up the "paddle." Much of the technique of arm action is designed to make the hand and forearm a more effective paddle. It's useful to look upon your hand as the "blade of the oar." The hands get into action early and effectively. They make the immediate contribution to propulsion.

As the stroke progresses and the forearms approach the vertical, their contribution becomes greater. The more up-and-down the forearms are, the more directly they can drive the water backward—and, therefore, the more they contribute to forward propulsion.

A good way to look at the arm action is to follow it from glide to glide. In this way we can see a complete cycle. Suppose we start with the glide. (We have to mention the word *glide* with a little caution, because many of the new greats are doing away with the full traditional glide, but more about that later.) As the legs begin their drive, the arms move forward together. The arms become straight and parallel to each other. When we watch the extension of the arms from the side, we see that they don't move exactly parallel to the surface of the water. Instead, the hands move somewhat downward so that at the end of the arm thrust the hands are about six to eight inches below the surface.

The forward movement of the arms accomplishes two main purposes. The arms reach a position from which they can begin another stroke, and when the arms are parallel to each other and close together, the body is streamlined. This streamlining helps to make the most of the forward drive supplied by the kick.

When the arms are fully forward, the hands are almost together and are about six or eight inches below the surface of the water. The first movement of the hands is outward and downward. The hands are allowed to "knife" through the water; that is, the first spreading and downward movement is carried out easily and without pressure. As the hands begin to move apart, the wrists are rotated so that the thumbs tend to drop.

The catch occurs at the point where the hands feel backward pressure against the water. The feeling can be compared with that of pulling an oar in a rowboat. You can feel the blade of the oar grab the water. It is important that the catch be made early in the stroke. In this way the pull is lengthened. An early catch is brought about by both correct rotation of the wrists and speed of the arms.

Just after the catch is made, the elbows begin to bend and the arms start to rotate inwardly. The elbows are kept high. A high position of the elbows is critical to an effective stroke. The inward rotation of the arms and the high position of the elbows allow the hands and forearms to push directly backward. The palms of the hands are toward the rear, and the forearms are nearly vertical. The action of the stroke is rapid. The hands and forearms move backward as fast as possible. Only a fast stroke can contribute to forward propulsion. A single slow stroke would cause drag or water resistance.

Although the hands and forearms form the "blade," the muscles of the upper body are the real source of power. In general, the stronger the upper body, the faster the "blades" can be moved through the water. That's why we will be talking about special exercises designed to strengthen the muscles of the upper body.

The pull ends at the shoulders. Coaches always emphasize this point, because they find that swimmers tend to think that they can gain something extra by using a longer arm action. It doesn't work. The stroke is much more efficient when it ends at the shoulders. The stroke is short and fast primarily because it must be timed with a single kick. Arm action must be carried out quickly. Except for the first stroke following the start and the turn, there is no time for the full stroke and follow-through that is characteristic of the other competitive strokes.

The completion of the stroke blends smoothly and quickly into the recovery action. As the pull finishes at the shoulders, the hands come together and then continue to move quickly forward into a streamlined position. The arms are close together. They are not quite parallel to the surface of the water, since the hands are about six to eight inches deep. The position of the arms helps streamline the body and hence takes advantage of the kick. When carried out well, the transition from pull to recovery is hardly noticeable. It looks like a single continuous act—a smooth, flowing motion. There should be no pause between the finish of the pull and the recovery.

Breathing. The need to breathe always interferes to some extent with the streamlining of the body and hence has some tendency to reduce speed. The task is to breathe in such a way that the interference with forward propulsion is minimal. Various methods of taking a breath have been tried. Some fine swimmers have simply kept their heads up at all times and in this way could breathe whenever they wanted to. Yet both research and expert opinion make it clear that this method is inefficient. With the head always raised, you can't achieve your best streamlining.

We do know that raising the head makes it difficult to keep your best body position. So we can safely assume two principles. First, the head should be raised only as high as is needed to take in a breath. Second, the time that the head is raised should be kept to a minimum. That is, the head should get back in the water as quickly as possible so that the best streamlining of the body can be resumed.

When should the head be raised to take a breath? You notice that this section on breathing is included in the chapter on arm action. That's because raising the head to breathe is timed with arm movement. The head starts to rise just after the arm pull has begun. At the completion of the pull, the head is raised to its highest point, and a breath is taken. Again, just after you start your pull your head begins to rise. As you finish your pull, you allow your head to reach its highest point. Breath is taken in quickly.

It's important to train yourself to raise your head just enough to take in a full gulp of air. Extra height causes needless drag. Once air has been taken in, your head is returned to the water as quickly as possible. There should be a conscious and vigorous action of the neck muscles. In making this strong and definite effort, however, do not let your head submerge completely.

Exhalation of air is both powerful and late. The air is held in your lungs until just before you are ready to inhale. The air is expelled all at once: At that point, when the air is vigorously driven out, the face is still in the water but just about to rise clear of the water. There is only a split second between exhalation and inhalation. It would, of course, be possible to eject the air from your lungs during almost any part of the stroke. The main purpose in holding the air so long is to maintain buoyancy. When the lungs are fully inflated, the body floats better. The body is higher in the water and can be moved more efficiently.

In working on your arm action you want to make your technique as efficient as possible and at the same time learn to stay within the rules. In actual swimming the arm action is never carried out in isolation. You can see that the movement of the arms is coordinated with breathing. And arm action is highly coordinated with leg action. We will be talking more about that.

1. The goal is efficient forward movement, so the pull of the arms is as directly backward as possible, backward action producing forward reaction.

1a

1b

1c

1d

1e

2. A full cycle of arm action seen from poolside. From a position of recovery (*a*) the hands move apart (*b*) and the recovery is made (*c*, *d*, and *e*). The pull ends when the hands get back as far as the shoulders (*f*). The arms continue in smooth motion to effect the recovery (*g*, *h*, and *i*).

2a

2c

2d

2f

2g

2i

2b

2e

2h

3. Recovery begins. The hands come together to reduce water resistance.

4. Head-on underwater shots of arm action. During recovery (*a* and *b*) the hands move forward *below* the surface of the water. The high elbows (*e*) are essential to an effective pull. The forearms are almost vertical.

4*a*

4*d*

4*e*

4*h*

4*i*

4b

4c

4f

4g

5a

5. After recovery, the hands are close together (*a*). They start to turn outward (*b*) and the catch is made (*c*).

5b

5c

6. Breathing is timed with arm action. The head gradually rises during the arm pull (*a*) and emerges at the completion of the pull (*b* and *c*). Air is quickly taken in. The head is back in the water for recovery (*d*) and the start of the stroke (*e*). The cycle of pull and breathing continues (*f–i*).

6*a*

6*d*

6*e*

6*h*

6*i*

6b

6c

6f

6g

The Kick

The breaststroke kick is interesting, significant, and different. Interesting, because its mechanics present a fascinating challenge. Significant, because the kick makes a greater contribution to propulsion than does the leg action of any other stroke. Different, because it involves a rotary or lateral sweep of the legs, whereas the leg action of the other strokes is up and down. To put it another way, the breaststroke kick takes place in a horizontal plane, while the kicks of the other strokes are carried out in the vertical plane.

Some experts contend that the kick is not important in sprint crawl swimming, but all experts recognize the great importance of the kick in the breaststroke. Some freestylers have performed well with an inadequate kick. Not so with the breaststrokers. All serious breaststrokers must develop highly effective leg action.

When we talked about arm action, we started with the rules. In considering the kick we have to do the same thing. About the action of the legs the rules specify that:

The feet shall be drawn up simultaneously and symmetrically, the knees bent and open. The movement shall be continued with a round and outward sweep of the feet, bringing the legs together. Up and down movements of the legs in the vertical plane are prohibited. Breaking water surface with the feet shall not merit disqualification unless caused by movement of the legs in a vertical plane.

What the rules really amount to is that the action of one leg must look like the mirror image of the other, and you can't kick up and down. Actually, the rules should not present a problem. It should be relatively easy for you to develop and ingrain a kicking pattern that will be well within the rules.

An overall look at the kick. The leg action has two basic parts. There is the recovery, or preparation to strike, and the actual kick itself. Looking at the gross action, we see that during recovery the legs flex or bend. There is a flexion at the hips and a bending of the knees. The main thrust of the kick comes about by a vigorous straightening of the legs. In making the kick, the goal is to build up speed of the feet and at the same time make the direction of thrust as directly backward as possible. The cycle of leg action, then, is recovery and thrust—or flex and straighten. Let's take a look at some of the details of leg action and the reasons for them.

Recovery. The purpose of the recovery is, of course, to get the legs into a position from which an effective kick can be made. Since kicking is continuous, we can start anywhere, but it seems useful to start by looking at the glide. During the glide the legs are extended straight back in a streamlined position. The streamlining is further improved by relaxing the ankles and thus allowing the toes to point backward.

Recovery starts from the glide position. The knees bend and the hips flex. The bend at the knees is extreme, the lower legs reaching about a vertical position. The heels are brought fairly close to the buttocks. This full flexion at the knees gets you ready for a powerful backward thrust against the water.

When we look at the recovery action of the legs from the rear, we can see that the feet never get very far apart. The distance between the feet should not be more than the width of the hips. By keeping the feet somewhat close together you reduce drag or water resistance. As the full bend of the knees is reached, the feet are turned and flexed. The toes point outward and slightly downward. In this way the feet are positioned to act as a better "paddle."

During the recovery of the legs, flexion at the hips goes on at the same time as flexion at the knees. But the bend at the hips is not so extreme. Although an extreme bend at the hips would create more potential for power, it would also create more drag or water resistance. Hence, you try to reach the best compromise between power and water resistance. This compromise results in a partial bend of the legs at the hips. The photos will give you a good idea of the right amount of bend.

The flexion at the hips is needed for kick power. The bend definitely has to be made, but you have to be aware that this action drops the upper leg and does cause considerable water resistance. In other words, the lowering of the knee is a negative factor that tends to slow you down. The solution is to maintain this flexed position at the hips for the shortest possible amount of time. Move your legs into this position as quickly as you can and then get right out of the position. The action should be both continuous and fast.

The Kick. A good kick has three important aspects. First, you want to build up to the greatest possible speed of the feet. The feet have to be moving quickly to make a contribution to forward propulsion. Second, the main thrust or action should be backward so that the reaction can be forward. Third, the feet must be positioned in a way that forms the most effective "paddle."

The pattern of the kicking action is both backward and circular. The backward action is best seen by looking at the kick from a side view. From the flexed position of the recovery, the legs drive backward until they are straight. Drive is made by the powerful muscles of the hips and upper legs. Correct positioning of the feet depends primarily upon the looseness of the ankles. During the kick, flexion of the feet involves two planes. There is rotation at the ankle so that the toes tend to point outward, or away from each other. That is, the right foot tends to point to the right and the left foot to the left. At the same time, the toes move inward toward the shinbone. This movement is the significant one as far as backward thrust is concerned, because the soles of the feet become positioned to drive the water backward more directly. When the backward push is completed, the ankle flexes so that the toes are pointing toward the rear. This movement adds power and improves streamlining of the feet to take advantage of the glide.

Although the emphasis of the kick is on backward thrust, the action is also rounded. We can best see this rounded action from a rear view. The kick is started from a position in which the feet are fairly close together. During the kick the feet spread apart and finally finish together again. We talked about two types of foot movement that are important to a good kick. The outward movement of the feet, in which they tend to point away from each other, is highly important to the circular aspect of the kick. The feet become more efficient "paddles." In this way the feet catch a lot of water and drive it backward. The circular movement also extends the "paddle" to include the forelegs.

You can see that the looser your ankles, the better you can kick. It's a big advantage to be naturally loose, but if you're not, special exercises to increase flexibility should be an essential part of your work-out schedule.

Coordination of arms and legs. The actions of the arms and legs are timed with each other so as to produce a continuous application of power. The more evenly power is applied, the more efficient the propulsion. For this reason the arm pull alternates with the kick.

Let's follow a full cycle of arm pull and kick, starting with the glide. During the brief moment of the glide, emphasis is on a streamlined position. The body is flat or close to the horizontal plane. The legs are straight, with the toes pointing to the rear. The arms are extended forward, with the hands close together. The pull starts. During the pull, the legs remain straight and streamlined. As the pull is completed, the legs start to bend to begin their recovery. At the same time, the arms continue to move toward recovery position.

When the kick begins, the arms are already well forward. The arms finish their extension during the completion of the kick. You are then back to the full glide position and ready for another cycle.

Even though it is held for only a fraction of a second, the glide has been a characteristic and attractive feature of breaststroke swimming. Yet some experts think that the glide will disappear—even in the 200-meter race. They feel that continuous action will produce greater speed. It seems logical enough that the elimination of the glide could increase swimming speed, but, if so, even greater physical conditioning is going to be needed.

As you progress in mastering the breaststroke, you may want to experiment with continuous stroke action. However, it seems best to use a glide while establishing your fundamentals.

7. A dry-land demonstration of the kick. In the glide position (*a*) the legs are streamlined to reduce drag. Flexion of the legs starts (*b*) and continues until recovery is complete (*d*). Having recovered, the legs start their powerful thrust (*e*). Ankles turn so that the toes point outward. Action is both circular and outward and is completed when the legs again reach a streamlined position.

7a

7d

7e

7h

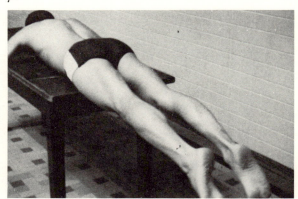

7i

8. During the recovery of the legs, two flexions take place. There is a bend at the knees and a bend at the hips. The amount of flexion at the hips represents a compromise, since bend produces both greater potential for power and greater water resistance. The optimum amount of bend is shown (*d* and *e*). Since flexion creates drag, the action should be carried out quickly.

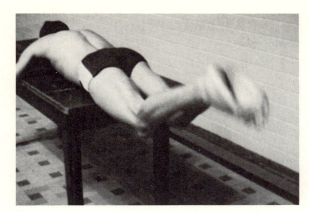

7b

7c

7f

7g

8a

8b

8c

8d

8g

8h

9. An underwater sequence demonstrating coordination of arm and leg action. As the arms pull (*a–d*), the legs keep their streamlined position. With the completion of the arm pull (*e*) the legs begin their recovery. The legs begin their powerful outward and backward thrust and again reach streamlined position (*n*).

9a

9d

9e

8e

8f

9b

9c

9f

9g

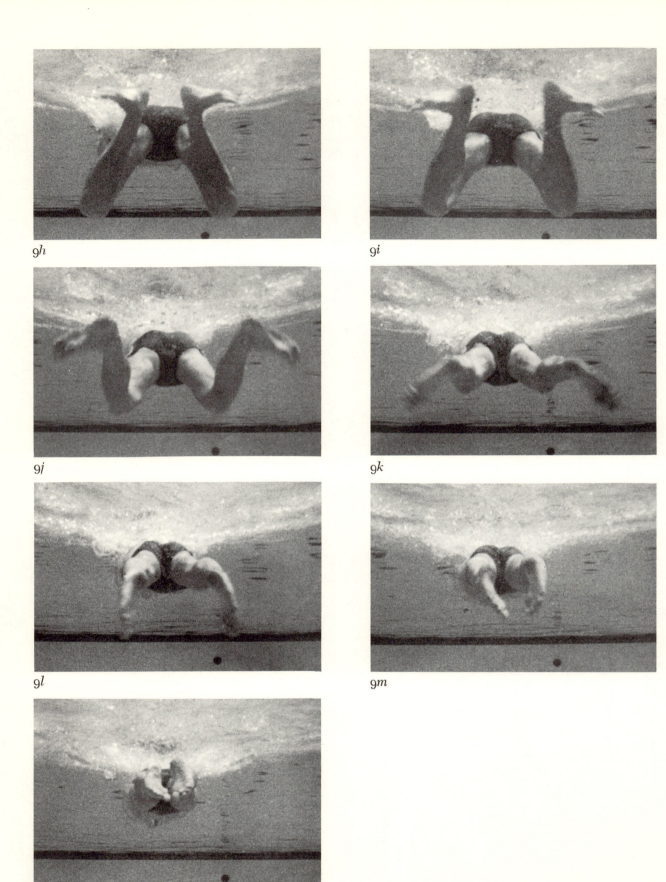

9*h*

9*i*

9*j*

9*k*

9*l*

9*m*

9*n*

The Start

The techniques used in starting the breaststroke race are almost the same as those used in the freestyle start. Hence, any practice time you may have spent learning an efficient start for the freestyle will be put to good use in perfecting the breaststroke start. The only real difference between the two starts is that the breaststroker enters the water at a slighly larger angle. This steeper angle puts the breaststroker deeper in the water. In this way he can remain under water long enough to take advantage of the rules that permit him to take one full arm pull and one kick before rising to the surface. This point is significant and we will be talking about it later in this section.

Goals of the start. Before reviewing the mechanics of the start, let's see what you want to accomplish. First, you want to be able to move quickly at the sound of the gun. Your ability to react to the gun will depend upon your inherent reaction time, your training, and your concentration. Second, maximum power off the mark is important. The greater the power off the platform the farther forward you will be when you hit the water, and the faster you will be moving. The amount of power you can develop will depend upon your strength and speed and the efficiency of your form. Third, you want to enter the water in a streamlined body position that will make the most of the momentum that you have developed. And fourth, you want to reach an underwater position that is streamlined and at the right depth to carry out the next moves.

On the platform. A starting position is taken on the platform with the feet slightly apart. A distance of from six inches to a foot seems about right for most swimmers. The toes curl over the forward edge of the platform. At "Take your mark" there is a partial bend of the knees and a crouch forward. Body weight is comfortably balanced over the balls of the feet. The arms hang loosely. There is full concentration—on movement, not on the sound of the gun. If you think of movement rather than sound, you will react faster when the gun goes off.

At the gun. When the gun sounds, the body tilts forward. At the same time the arms begin a full and vigorous circular swing. The swing takes the arms upward and outward. During the first part of the swing, the hands are outward and away from the body. As the arms descend to complete their rotation, they move inward so that the hands pass close to the legs.

The arm swing and the body movement start together at the gun. During the arm swing, the body continues its movement downward and forward. The legs remain bent. The feet keep contact with the starting platform. As the arms pass the vertical, or lowest point, and begin to start upward, the powerful leg drive is begun. Just before the arms reach a horizontal position their movement is abruptly checked. The fast-moving arms have built up considerable energy, and thus the stopping of the arms causes their energy to be transferred to the body. In this way the forward speed of the body is increased. The legs complete their drive just as the body is almost parallel to the surface of the water.

Timing is vital in making the most of the leg drive to produce maximum forward speed. Yet timing is not that difficult to master. It simply takes patience to wait until the body lowers before making the leg drive against the platform.

Entering the water. The powerful thrust of the start develops speed. The body is moving fast, and the water should be entered in the way that best preserves this speed. The goal is a knifelike entry with the body as straight as possible. Any protrusion of the body would create water resistance and loss of valuable speed. The arms are forward and straight and in alignment with the body. Face is downward, with the head tucked between the arms.

Glide. When you enter the water, you actually have more speed than you can generate by swimming. It's important to take advantage of this speed by maintaining a streamlined body position upon entry. If you try to start swimming too soon, you will slow down. This is the time for patience and poise. The beginner is naturally anxious to rise to the surface immediately and get going. In contrast, the experienced swimmer remains calm. He makes full use of the speed afforded by the start. And, just as important, he does not rush to the surface. He remains under water long enough to take advantage of the arm pull and kick that the rules permit him to take.

It's clear enough that the arm pull starts when the initial speed supplied by the drive from the platform slows down to swimming speed. To know when this point is reached takes experience and some judgment. When an error is made it is almost always on the side of starting the arm pull too soon. Again, emphasis is on patience and poise.

During the glide your arms are straight ahead, and so they are already in position to start the pull when the time is ripe. The first part of the pull is just like that of a normal arm stroke. So all that you have been practicing to polish your regular arm pull applies. The difference is in the length of the pull. In the regular stroke the pull ends at the shoulders. In contrast, the underwater arm stroke is full. The thrust is all the way back until the arms are straight and the hands are against the thighs.

During the arm pull the legs remain straight and streamlined, to make the most of the thrust generated by the arms. The legs begin their recovery. The recovery is like that used in normal swimming. The same techniques are used, with, of course, the same emphasis on speed of recovery. The arms continue their own recovery, with the hands moving very close to the body in order to cut down on water resistance.

The kick is made with the arms straight out and the hands slightly below the surface of the water—the same position that you have been using in the normal stroke. The streamlining of the arms helps take full advantage of the power supplied by the kick. The rules state that you cannot begin your second stroke until a part of the head breaks the surface of the water. So you can see the ideal timing. You want to get in your underwater arm pull and kick and reach the surface just as you are ready for your next stroke. Efficient timing takes practice and experience.

The "grab" start. In the next few years there could be an important change in starting technique. As you know, in track the sprinter starts from a crouched position. Except for getting off the mark quickly, the tasks of the sprinter and swimmer are somewhat different. For the runner the crouch helps bring his center of gravity forward, and in this way there is more efficient acceleration. The advantage the crouch start might offer the swimmer is to get him in the water more quickly.

In the presently used starting technique the swimmer does not complete his leg drive from the platform until his body reaches a position almost parallel to the surface of the water. The swimmer has to wait for his leg drive until gravity lowers his body to a horizontal position. However, this interval is not completely wasted. During the lowering of the body the arm swing builds up energy that is used to help drive the body forward. The theory of the crouch or "grab" start is that because the body is poised in a lower position, the leg drive can be made sooner. In this way the interval from the sound of the gun to the entry would be shortened.

The theoretical advantages claimed for the "grab" start do seem reasonable. This start certainly should put you in the water sooner. However, it may be that other advantages are lost. The traditional start, though it may delay entry, may offer both greater distance and greater velocity. In other words, by using the traditional start you may be later in reaching the water, but you may make up the difference by being farther out and moving faster.

In any case it would be a good idea to keep an eye on experimentation with the "grab" start. Some of the outstanding swimmers are trying it. Scientifically minded coaches are testing this new start, so there should soon be an answer.

10. A solid base is needed for an effective start. The toes are curled securely around the edge of the platform.

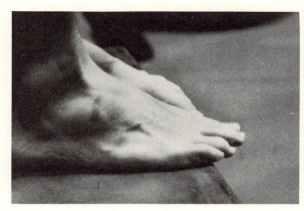

10*a*

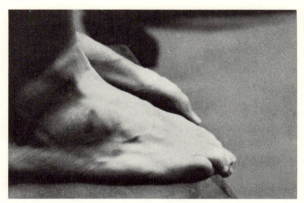

10*b*

11. Ready for the gun, you are crouched forward, relaxed and balanced. At the sound of the gun the body moves forward and downward and, at the same time, the arms start their rotation upward and outward. As the arms descend they come close to the body. Trace their pattern. The arms coordinate with the legs so that their momentum adds to the leg drive from the platform. The body is almost parallel to the surface of the water as the final leg push is made. Entry is knifelike to conserve momentum.

11*a*

11*d*

11*e*

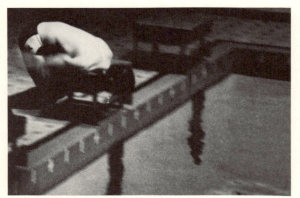

11*h*

11*i*

11*l*

11*m*

11b

11c

11f

11g

11j

11k

12. You enter the water with great speed.

12a

13. Entry is deeper than in other strokes and patience is needed to take advantage of initial momentum (*a*). When the arm pull is made, it is full (*b–e*).

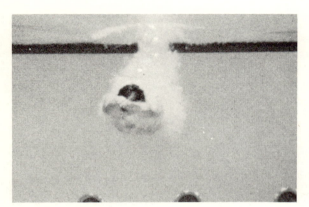

13a

13b

13e

14. The full effort of the first stroke brings the hands to the thighs. The arms and legs recover together.

14c

14d

12b

13c

13d

14a

14b

14e

14f

The Turn

It's easy to see the great importance of the turn. Many championships are decided by the ability to turn well. You will often see a race in which two swimmers approach the wall on even terms, but coming off the wall, one of them has a lead. And the lead increases with each turn. The swimmer who has developed a fast and efficient turn obviously has a great advantage.

The task is to get off the wall quickly and with power. But, as in all aspects of the breaststroke, observation of the rules is the prime consideration. You work to develop a technique that is within the rules so that you don't have to worry about disqualification.

The rules for the turn are simple. The touch of the wall has to be made with both hands at the same time and at the same level. The shoulders must be horizontal. Once the touch of the wall has been made, you are free to turn in any way you want. But before leaving the wall you must return to the breaststroke form. Your last contact with the wall will be with your feet, and just before that contact is broken you have to be back on your breast. The rules are clear enough. The job, however, is to ingrain your turn so thoroughly that it will be carried out within the rules under the stress and excitement of competition.

Approaching the wall. The timing of the approach to the wall is less of a problem than it is in the other strokes. The breaststroker has the advantage of being able to see the wall better. Thus, he can control stroke length so as to reach the wall at the best time. The ideal time to reach the wall is just as the kick has been completed. At this point the glide is at its fastest, and the arms are stretched forward in a position to make contact with the wall.

When your hands make contact with the wall, ideally you should grasp something that would afford leverage for both lifting and turning your body. A gutter is best, because it is easily grasped and at about the right height for the efficient use of your arms. But many pools have gutters only at the sides and not at the ends. If there is no gutter, the next best bet is the deck of the pool. Use the deck if it is low enough for you to reach it readily. It is possible that you will compete in a pool that lacks a gutter and has a very high deck. In such a case your hand contact would have to be against a flat wall. So that you won't be caught unprepared, it's a good idea to practice your turn under all three of the conditions you might meet.

Action at the wall. When your hands make contact with the wall, the arms give or bend slightly. You can plan to turn either to the right or to the left. The direction of turn is a matter of what seems natural to you. But for the moment let's assume that you are going to turn to your right.

Just after the arms bend slightly on contact, several events take place at the same time. The arms are depressed to lift the body. Emphasis is on the left hand, because the right hand is getting ready for a whip to the right. The action of the left arm can lift the body sufficiently, and, because the lift comes from one side of the body, rotation is initiated. In other words, the left arm should do most of the lifting work. Acting alone, the left arm can easily raise the body as high as it should be raised. And the stronger action of one arm tends to impart a spinning action to the body.

Arm action is coordinated with action of the legs. The job of the legs is to make quick and firm contact with the wall and at the right level. Upon contact with the wall the legs start to tuck. The tighter the tuck, the more easily and faster the body turns. The tuck serves still another purpose. It helps bring the legs to the right height for the push-off against the wall. The legs are also lifted by the downward pressing action of the left arm.

As the legs are positioning for a powerful push, the arm action continues. The left arm makes a hard drive against the wall, both to help turn the body and to give it forward momentum. At the same time the right arm leaves the wall and whips around so that the hand moves toward the chest. When the left arm completes its pushing and turning effort off the wall, its movement brings the left hand to the chest. Both arms are then ready to move forward into glide position. The head is submerged and then placed between the arms to improve streamlining.

As you would expect, the lifting of the head during the turn gives the breaststroker a chance to take in a full breath. There is still another bonus. At the completion of the push against the wall, the upper body drops to submerge. Since at this point gravity is doing the work, the swimmer takes a split second of relaxation. The great breaststrokers report that this brief respite is important to them.

The leg drive off the wall is all-important, because the effectiveness of the drive determines the speed at which you leave. Hence, in making your turn, an essential point of technique in carrying out the spin is to wind up with both feet in a solid driving position against the wall. The feet are about two feet below the surface and slightly apart. The push is powerful and full. The body is streamlined to take advantage of the leg drive off the wall.

Leaving the wall. After the legs finish their drive, you have exactly the same situation and the same rules that you have in the start. Compliance with the rules is the first consideration. The first rule is that you be back in breaststroke position when you leave the wall. As soon as the feet break contact with the wall, you have to be back on your breast. But that should not be much of a problem. It just takes some practice. Then you can give concentration to making the best possible use of initial speed and the single stroke and single kick that the rules allow.

A good push off the wall creates more speed than does swimming. As you leave the wall you are at your fastest. This simple fact tends to be easily forgotten in the excitement of a race. There is a natural and understandable anxiety to "get going." But efforts to swim too soon actually slow you down. And premature swimming also wastes valuable energy. The right time to start swimming is when the speed generated by the powerful drive off the wall slows down to swimming speed. It takes judgment to know the right moment to start swimming. It also takes practice and patience.

You will recall that the start of the breaststroke is deeper than the starts for other strokes. So it is with the turn. Coming off the turn, you drive deep enough so that you will be under water long enough to take the single pull and single kick that the rules allow you to take beneath the surface.

The single underwater pull is somewhat different from the regular stroke made during surface swimming. Unlike the regular breaststroke action in which the stroke ends at the shoulders, the underwater stroke is full. The arms continue to pull until they are extended with the hands along the thighs. The full pull under water is the most powerful stroke of the race.

At the finish of the stroke streamlining is maintained. Because of the great speed generated by a powerful push off the wall, a gliding position is held longer than the regular glide of normal swimming. Arms are at the sides and the legs are straight. The timing of recovery is different from the recovery of surface strokes. After the right amount of delay to take advantage of the speed produced by the drive off the wall, recovery of the arms and legs takes place at the same time. The arms move forward along the body and stretch forward until they are in a streamlined position. The legs recover and strike. Streamlined body position is held. Just as the head breaks the surface of the water, the pull is started. This timing between the emergence of the head and the start of the second stroke is vital because of the rules. On this point the rules are exactly the same as they are for the start.

The details of the turn are highly important. They have to be understood and mastered. But all the details of form have to be put together to make for a smooth and coordinated act. The turn should appear as a single flow of motion. And, of course, the turn must be fast. An important first step is to get the clearest possible mental image of the turn. Then keep working to perfect it. Even when your turn seems satisfactory, don't take it for granted. Keep working at it. A qualified observer is always helpful, and your own coach is your best observer.

15. The turn is a vital part of your race. You can gain speed through an efficient and powerful turn because the wall supplies a base for greater speed than the water can offer.

15a

15d

16. The breaststroker can see the wall and hit it at his best speed, just as he finishes his kick (*a* and *b*). To keep within the rules, both hands touch the wall at the same time with the shoulders horizontal (*c* and *d*). The gutter or deck is grasped (*e*), and the body is lifted and turned (*f–i*). While the upper body turns, the legs seek a power position on the wall (*j–m*). The drive off the wall (*n*) has to be timed so that the swimmer is once more back to a horizontal position.

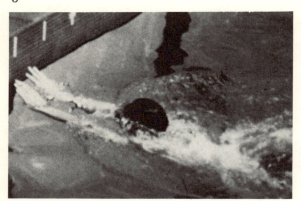

16c

16d

16g

16h

15b

15c

16a

16b

16e

16f

16i

16j

16k

16l

17a

17. Power off the wall comes from two sources, the arms (*a* and *b*) and the legs (*c*, *d*, and *e*).

17d

17e

18b

16m

16n

17b

17c

18a

18. The second stroke is taken as the head breaks the surface.

18c

18d

V. Training

In determining your day-to-day workout programs there is no substitute for an experienced and dedicated coach. Your coach will help you in many ways, but one of his most critical contributions to your success will be the work schedules that he gives you. In designing your programs he can take account of many factors that especially apply to you.

Your coach naturally expects your full cooperation, but he doesn't want you to work blindly. He knows that your enthusiasm will be greater and your progress faster if you understand some of the "whys" of what is being done. In brief, your understanding of conditioning and training methods is not for the purpose of second-guessing your coach. Instead, such an understanding will help you profit more from coaching instruction.

Goals. Your training schedule is designed to accomplish three main goals. You will want to improve techniques including starts and turns. You will want to become faster. And you will want to build great endurance. These three goals are related to each other. Work designed to reach one goal also helps reach the others.

Perfecting technique is an ongoing process. Your form will get continuous attention from you and your coach. You will work especially to ingrain efficient form to the point that it becomes almost instinct. In this way your form will be solid enough to hold up under the conditions of stress and fatigue that you can expect in a race. There is no conflict between working on technique and any other goal. You can and should be conscious of form even if the primary goal of the moment is speed or endurance.

A sprinter must, of course, include lots of speed work in the schedule. In general, speed depends on the amount of power that is developed and the efficiency with which the power is applied. A great deal of fast swimming builds power. At the same time, fast swimming affords practice in carrying out techniques under conditions of high speed.

All training goals are important, but the most significant aspect of modern training methods has been the building of greater endurance. Today's swimmers are much better conditioned than those of a generation ago.

Rationale. Within certain limits the body has a remarkable ability to adjust to the task given to it. This is the basic fact that underlies training and conditioning methods in swimming and other sports.

The word "task" is highly significant. The task given to the body in training depends upon the nature of the event. In addition to specific skills, most sports require both strength and endurance. The ratios of these two factors can vary from one sport to another. There are extremes. For example, in track and field the shot-putter's physical needs contrast with those of the distance runner. The shot-putter is concerned almost entirely with strength. His performance depends on a quick burst of power. At the other end of the scale, the distance runner's ability to perform depends primarily on his endurance. Obviously, the workout goals and therefore schedules of the two athletes will be very different. In planning his training program the shot-putter will give his body the primary task of building great strength. The distance runner's program will be designed to develop great endurance.

Regardless of the task the body must be given a chance to adjust. Both time and spacing are needed. The work load is gradually increased. In other words, the training is "progressive." In this way the body gets used to the task and is able to make the needed changes or adjustments.

Great sprinters are always very strong athletes. That figures, because sprinting requires great power. But the sprinter also needs enormous endurance. In terms of energy output over a time period, a one-hundred-yard swim is about equivalent to running 440 yards.

In recent times all sports where measurement is available have had record explosions. In no sport has the record explosion been more spectacular than in swimming. The "secret" of the explosion has been greatly increased work. There was a time when the swimmer "perfected" his style and then afterward barely practiced between competitions. During the first part of the twentieth century it was discovered that conditioning could bring about enormous advantages. Records started to fall. It became clear that the athlete who worked hard in practice to get in shape performed much better. The famous Yale coach, Bob Kiphuth, was a highly influential pioneer in this effort. Coach Kiphuth's emphasis on the idea of work produced a long series of great Yale teams.

In this half of the twentieth century the need to work hard in practice has been increasingly emphasized. More and more mileage is being swum. Two related scientific efforts have been underway. There is an attempt to find out the optimum amount of practice work and the ways that the work should be carried out so that the body can best profit from it. The first problem still remains somewhat subjective. Experienced coaches are needed to figure out the point at which a swimmer has had the right amount of work. As for applying the "doses" of work, science and trial and error have produced some truly effective methods.

The common denominator of all good workout programs is work itself. But in setting up a specific workout there are infinite possibilities. That's because of the variables that lend themselves to different combinations. There is the distance to be swum, the pace or time, the number of repetitions or times the distance is swum, and the amount of rest taken between repetitions.

Interval Training and Repetition Training. These two terms will become increasingly familiar to you. The methods are somewhat similar, but there are important differences. Both involve the four basic variables that have been mentioned. For example, under either method part of the day's work might be swimming one hundred yards ten times (10 × 100). However, there are two related differences between interval training and repetition training. These differences involve the length of the rest interval between repetitions and usually the speed at which a repetition is swum. Concerning the rest interval, central to interval training is the idea that recovery from the previous repetition should not be complete before doing the next one. Your rest will be very short so that your heart rate will still be fast. In contrast, repetition training calls for a rest interval long enough for almost complete recovery. Heart rate approaches normal, and you breathe without difficulty.

Because repetition training gives you more time to rest between repeats, the repetitions are usually faster than in interval training. In repetition training a portion of the race is selected as the repeat. This section is swum somewhat faster than it would be in the race. The same is seldom true for interval training, because recovery from previous repeats is not complete. To increase the pace in interval training, either the rest intervals would have to be longer or the distance of the repeats shorter.

Both systems, interval training and repetition training, can provide for an infinite variety of workout programs. In addition, there are other methods of training that your coach will prescribe from time to time. Regardless of the methods used you can expect to do a lot of work. The body adjusts, but no more than it has to. The only way it can get used to a lot of work is to do a lot of work.

Land Exercises. Great competitive swimming requires both endurance and strength. The best and most direct way to develop swimming endurance is by doing enough swimming. Interval training, repetition training, and other methods are designed to build endurance. As for strength, however, it was discovered that it can be developed faster by means of land exercises.

Swimmers use a vast variety of exercises. There are literally hundreds in use. Most of them fall into one of four categories—weight training, isometrics, apparatus work, and calisthenics. The basic idea in strength building is to increase gradually the work load of the muscles. The muscles adjust to greater work and become stronger. Systematic increases are essential. The muscles will only adjust to the work given to them.

Nearly all exercises tend to have value. However, weight training offers an important advantage. The resistance of each exercise can be conveniently increased and accurately measured. In this way weight training permits almost optimum schedules.

A general weight-training program can develop all-round strength, but you've got to keep in mind your basic goal—that of becoming a fine swimmer. Under the guidance of your coach you will want to set up a program that is specifically designed to improve swimming. Such a program will emphasize development of the muscles that make the major contributions to propulsion through the water. To build up muscles that add nothing to the swimming effort can actually hamper performance. Endurance can be reduced.

Your coach may prescribe isometric exercises. These are different from other exercises in that the muscles contract without bodily movement. When carried out against an immovable object the amount of resistance cannot be measured. However, isometrics do have some advantages. A critical point in a stroke movement can be isolated and given special attention. Hence isometrics can be used both to build muscle and to aid the learning process.

You don't have to be an expert on land exercises, but the more you understand the importance of this training, the more enthusiasm you will have for it. And the more cooperation you will give your coach.

Kickboard and Leg-tied Drills. Most of the yardage you cover in the pool will be with normal swimming. However, most coaches add two special drills. You will be asked to kick certain distances with a kickboard. Also, you will be asked to swim with your legs tied. When you use a kickboard, your legs supply the entire propulsion, and when you tie your legs, the arms must do all of the work.

Each drill has two basic purposes. In using the kickboard the legs receive more stress than they would in normal swimming. The overload builds strength and endurance. Also the efficiency of leg action receives more attention. The efficiency of this action can be examined and corrections can be made. The same purposes are served by tying the legs. The arms get more work than they ordinarily would, and their action can get special attention.

Picking your event. You may have already gravitated toward the free-style events. Even though this style might be your first preference and your best event, it pays to learn the other three competitive strokes—backstroke, butterfly, and breaststroke. You cannot be sure where your best aptitude lies until you've given each stroke a try. You will get a lot of satisfaction from mastering the other strokes, and there will be times when you can bring in extra points that could mean victory for your team.

You may become either a sprinter or a distance swimmer. But, again, it's best to keep the option open. Experience, especially actual racing, will indicate your most natural distance. When your best distance does become clear your workout schedules will be shaped so as to emphasize either speed or distance.

Warm-up. Great athletes in all sports start each practice session with a thorough warm-up. They wouldn't think of doing otherwise. For some reason the beginner tends to view his warm-up as a mere ritual or nuisance. It takes him a while to realize that the warm-up is an essential part of his workout.

A great variety of warm-up routines can be effective. There is lots of room for experiment. However, for good reasons concerned with human nature the coach's instructions are usually specific. If there are specific things to do, even the novice tends to get an adequate warm-up. Most top swimmers cover about one thousand yards in warming up. They often start with a long swim of about four to five hundred yards. They follow this swim with shorter distances at faster speeds. Brief rests are taken between repeats. Beginners are usually instructed to follow a similar pattern but to swim less yardage.

Getting a warm-up at a large meet can pose some problems. The pool will be crowded, and there will be limited time. You and your coach will probably work out a warm-up routine that will depend heavily on land exercises.

Effect on Your Life. You probably already know that great success takes dedication and sacrifice. You cannot become an outstanding swimmer by taking a few dips in the pool and then doing anything else that you want. It is best to be realistic and know the price of achievement. The price includes discipline and hard work. There is no easy road.

No athlete can get in condition for championship swimming without subjecting himself to almost daily stress. There is no other way to do it. It is human and natural enough to reject punishment and pain. Only the unusual person can persevere to great swimming achievement.

After you accept the price of success, there are still other patterns you must take into consideration. You can surely understand the need to put great stress on your body. You know that's the way that your body becomes efficient and capable of performance. But since you are going to be under this calculated and profitable stress, you cannot also be placed under a lot of other stresses—emotional and otherwise. To the best of your ability you should try to streamline or regulate your life. You cannot afford to waste your energies and time.

The life of a champion has to be Spartan, but in ordering your life and using your time well you do not and should not exclude other worthwhile activities. The discipline that you derive from your training should carry over and help you in other activities. Many great swimmers continue to be honor students throughout college and then go on to distinguished professional or business careers.

You are going to work hard to become a fine swimmer. But you will feel more than rewarded by the joy of competition and the satisfaction of having done well.

1. Pullovers with relatively light weights are a basic weight training exercise for all swimmers. They can be carried out with either dumbells or a barbell.

1a

1b

1c

2. Bench presses strengthen both the pushing muscles of the arms and the muscles of the chest.

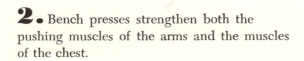

3. The bench press can be conveniently carried out on more advanced equipment, which is becoming increasingly available.

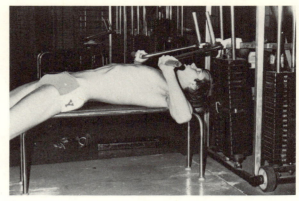

3a

4. The extensors or pushing muscles of the legs are strengthened on a machine. The same muscles can be exercised in a number of other ways, including knee bends or squats.

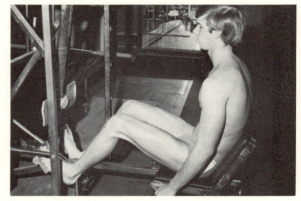

4a

5. Pulley weights were used for generations before weight training came into prominence. Still valuable, they provide measured resistance and also a high degree of flexibility. Important parts of the actual swimming motion can be simulated. In this way the muscles that most contribute to propulsion can be singled out for attention.

5a

5b

5e

5f

3b

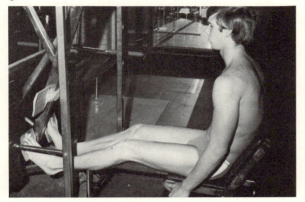

4b

5c

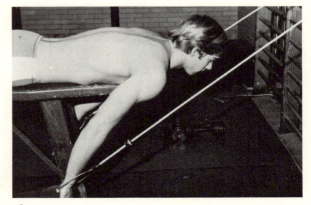

5d

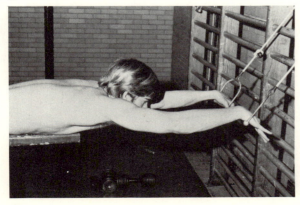

5g

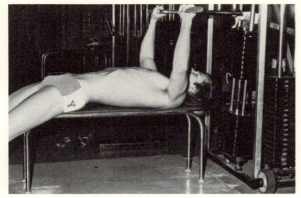

5h

6. With the legs tied, the arms have to do all the work and thereby develop greater strength and endurance. Also, arm action can be given special attention.

7. With the arms resting on a kickboard, the legs have to do all the work. They then get the benefits of isolation—strength, endurance, and attention to technique.

8. The great swimmers become "clock-watchers." Correct timing is needed to carry out the vital methods of interval training and repetition training.

8a

8b

Last Word

Our attempt has been to bring you the best information we can about swimming. The emphasis has been on the techniques and training methods that produce champions. Excellence in almost any activity is desirable and rewarding, whether that activity be poetry, mathematics, sports, or any of the wonderful things that mankind can do. But along the road to the goal of excellence there can be a lot of enjoyment. So it is with swimming. You can only gain in your efforts to do well.

A selection of books published by Penguin is listed on the following pages.

For a complete list of books available from Penguin in the United States, write to Dept. DG, Penguin Books, 299 Murray Hill Parkway, East Rutherford, New Jersey 07073.

For a complete list of books available from Penguin in Canada write to Penguin Books Canada Limited, 2801 John Street, Markham, Ontario L3R 1B4.

If you live in the British Isles, write to Dept. EP, Penguin Books Ltd, Harmondsworth, Middlesex.

THE QUICKEST WAY TO DRAW WELL

Frederic Taubes

This popular book gives a concise course for the student who wants to develop skills in drawing rapidly. The author gives detailed but easily understood instruction in basic good draftsmanship and materials, as well as a variety of special techniques, for the beginner, the Sunday artist, and even the practicing professional. Frederic Taubes covers figure, landscape, and still-life subjects; perspective; and composition from both classic and contemporary viewpoints. For those who want the shortest path to proficiency, this book provides all the necessary steps for further accomplishment in any medium.

SELLING WHAT YOU MAKE

Jane Wood

"Have you ever made anything by hand and enjoyed it? Would you rather make things than get a job? Or, did you already get a job, replacing the craft you do like with the security in the job you don't like now? If any of these questions intrigues you, then this is your book." So writes Jane Wood, who shows how to sell the things you make—at art fairs, to stores, to buyers, to wholesalers. She discusses pricing your work, presenting your work, and keeping records. Most of all, she gives the commercially unsophisticated craftsman the self-confidence to start getting paid for making the things he enjoys making.

GYMNASTICS FOR GIRLS

Dr. Frank Ryan

The most exciting event in the past Olympic games, women's gymnastics, has come into its own as one of the great sports of our time. It is also a breathtakingly beautiful sport, in which each competitor must demonstrate her skills in four unique and demanding categories: floor exercise, balance beam, uneven parallel bars, and the vault. In this book Dr. Frank Ryan tells you all you need to know about the fundamentals of gymnastics, about individual tumbling and dance skills, about control and precision, about the split-second timing of work on the uneven parallel bars, about the techniques of aggressive performance on the vault, and much more. The author also offers invaluable advice on the development of combinations that will enable the gymnast to devise her own routines. Illustrated with dozens of step-by-step photographs, this is the most comprehensive guide available for today's young student—and tomorrow's champion.

WEIGHT TRAINING

Dr. Frank Ryan

Weight training, as opposed to weight lifting, is an invaluable aid in preparing for almost every sport. The goal of weight training is to develop coordinated power—the ability of a muscle, group of muscles, the body itself, to go farther or longer, run faster or harder, jump higher or wider. Stressing the need for safety and protection from injuries, acclaimed sports expert Dr. Frank Ryan covers each step in the process of physical development and coordination through exercise with weights and shows how this process can lead to athletic excellence.

THE RUNNER'S HANDBOOK:
A COMPLETE FITNESS GUIDE FOR
MEN AND WOMEN ON THE RUN

Bob Glover and Jack Shepherd

Here is the indispensable guide, the (simple) secrets of success for all runners and would-be runners. Bob Glover's Run Easy Method adapts to beginners of all ages but will also benefit those at intermediate and more advanced levels. A veteran marathoner, Glover includes advice on competing in races up to and beyond the full 26.2-mile marathon distance, and he clarifies the sometimes confusing training methods and diets. He and Shepherd discuss the fine points of running style, of stretching exercises and weight training, selecting shoes and other equipment, preparing for weather and road conditions, avoiding injury when you can and coping with it when you can't (Glover claims firsthand knowledge of almost every injury that can strike a runner). They take a quick look at the new field of running and meditation and a longer look at the effects of running on the heart and lungs—information and advice garnered from many of the country's top running doctors. A guide to running spaces in more than 25 major American cities is also included.

HOW TO LOOK AT SOCCER

Don Kowet

Soccer means continuous action: eleven men on each side creating constant ebb and flow—no half-inning hiatus as in baseball, no pause to shift defensive and offensive units as in football, no momentary disengagement of gears as in ice hockey; just two forty-five-minute halves with only a ten-minute rest in between. Opposing teams move from one end of the field to the other—now attacking, now defending, now exploding into a stunning attempt at a goal. The purpose of all this dazzling whirl and flux is simple: to score more goals than the opponent. To accomplish that objective, players use skills and strategies best appreciated by the knowing spectator. *How to Look at Soccer*, fully illustrated with photographs and diagrams, shows you how to "read" the world's most popular game.

TANGRAM: THE ANCIENT CHINESE SHAPES GAME

Joost Elffers

Tangram, the thousand-year-old Chinese puzzle, is an exciting game that stimulates creativity and fantasy and can be played by either one person or a group. The game consists of seven pieces, formed by cutting a square in a certain way. With these geometric pieces, one can copy the examples of shapes illustrated in the book. This may sound easy enough, but as soon as one starts playing, it becomes obvious that Tangram presents a real and pleasurable challenge to one's skill and visual imagination. This edition, along with the plastic puzzle pieces attached, includes an introduction, a bibliography, and a mathematical section that examines the number of possible shapes that can be formed. There are over 1,600 examples with solutions.

Also for puzzle lovers from Penguin:

THE SECOND PENGUIN BOOK OF *THE TIMES* CROSSWORDS
THE THIRD PENGUIN BOOK OF *THE TIMES* CROSSWORDS
THE FOURTH PENGUIN BOOK OF *THE TIMES* CROSSWORDS
THE PENGUIN BOOK OF *SUNDAY TIMES* CROSSWORDS
THE SECOND PENGUIN BOOK OF *SUNDAY TIMES* CROSSWORDS
THE FOURTH PENGUIN BOOK OF *SUNDAY TIMES* CROSSWORDS
THE THIRD PENGUIN BOOK OF *SUNDAY TIMES* CROSSWORDS

THE PENGUIN BOOK OF KITES

David Pelham

The kite is now enjoying a world revival that has partly to do with its functional beauty and partly with its paradoxical quality of providing exercise *and* relaxation to both mind and body. This book is a comprehensive and thoroughly illustrated introduction to kites and kiting, covering in detail their history, their construction, and their flying. It contrasts the highly decorative models of the East with the more functional and aerodynamically efficient Western types. Over one hundred detailed and tested kite patterns are included, giving all the information required to build kites.

PENGUIN STEREO RECORD GUIDE
Second Edition

Edward Greenfield, Robert Layton, and Ivan March

Drawing on profound technical knowledge and on vast musical and historical learning, this newly revised and updated guide to recorded classical music deals with over four thousand discs, giving details of title, performers, record number, label, and price range. For record buyers in a hurry, a starring system (from one to three stars) is provided; while, for the enlightenment of browsers, there is a short but informative discussion of each record. Upon a few records of outstanding quality the authors have conferred a "rosette"—a special mark of admiration on their part. This edition has been updated with American selections. "The authors' scope and zeal are stunning, their standards of judgment and accuracy high . . . what an achievement"—*Sunday Times* (London). "The answer to a record-collecting browser's prayer"—*High Fidelity*.

THE PENGUIN BOOK OF PETS:
A PRACTICAL GUIDE TO ANIMAL-KEEPING

Emil P. Dolensek, D.V.M., and Barbara Burn
Photographs by Bruce Buchenholz

This complete guide to the art of pet ownership tells you which pets to choose from more than a hundred animals classified as *easy, difficult,* and *impossible*; where to find pets; how to care for them with food, housing, and medical treatment; and how to train and breed them. In addition, the authors give valuable advice on the care and releasing of orphaned or wounded wild animals, on free-roaming pets, and on controversial issues like neutering animals and importing exotic species.

DOCTOR IN THE ZOO

Bruce Buchenholz
Introduction by Cleveland Amory

Here for animal-lovers of all ages is a warmly appreciative look in pictures and in words at a young zoo doctor. The average day of Dr. Emil P. Dolensek, chief veterinarian of the New York Zoological Society (the Bronx Zoo), can involve anything from mending the broken arm of a baby gorilla to taking care of an undernourished Siberian tiger kitten. The medical challenges are great enough, but complicating them is the fact that most wild animals respond badly to handling and treatment, requiring infinite patience, love, and expertise. Photographs bring the reader into intimate contact with situations as they arise at the zoo and emphasize the drama, intensity, and warmth of Dr. Dolensek's daily contact with the animals he cares for and about.

In single volumes in The Viking Portable Library there have been gathered the very best work of individual authors or works of a period of literary history, writings that otherwise would be available only in separate volumes. These are not condensed versions, but rather selected masterworks assembled and introduced with critical essays by distinguished authorities. Over fifty volumes of The Viking Portable Library are now in print in paperback, making the cream of ancient and modern Western writing available to bring pleasure and instruction to the student and the general reader. An assortment of subjects follows:

William Blake

Cervantes

Geoffrey Chaucer

Samuel Coleridge

Stephen Crane

Dante

Ralph Waldo Emerson

William Faulkner

Edward Gibbon

Greek Historians

Nathaniel Hawthorne

Henry James

Thomas Jefferson

Machiavelli

Medieval Reader

Herman Melville

John Milton

North American Indian Reader

Plato

Edgar Allan Poe

Poets of the English Language (5 volumes)
MEDIEVAL AND RENAISSANCE POETS: LANGLAND TO SPENSER
ELIZABETHAN AND JACOBEAN POETS: MARLOWE TO MARVELL
RESTORATION AND AUGUSTAN POETS: MILTON TO GOLDSMITH
ROMANTIC POETS: BLAKE TO POE
VICTORIAN AND EDWARDIAN POETS: TENNYSON TO YEATS

François Rabelais

Renaissance Reader

Roman Reader

William Shakespeare

Jonathan Swift

Mark Twain

Voltaire

Walt Whitman

Oscar Wilde